CO-ALL-488

MLM
(Multi-level Marketing)

Garrett Adams

Made E-Z

3 4 5 6 7 8 9 10

This publication is designed to provide accurate and authoritative information in regard to subject matter covered. It is sold with the understanding that neither the publisher nor author is engaged in rendering legal, accounting, or other professional services. If legal advice or other expert assistance is required, the services of a competent professional should be sought. From: *A Declaration of Principles jointly adopted by a Committee of the American Bar Association and a Committee of Publishers.*

MLM Made E-Z™
Garrett Adams

Limited warranty and disclaimer

This self-help product is intended to be used by the consumer for his/her own benefit. It may not be reproduced in whole or in part, resold or used for commercial purposes without written permission from the publisher. In addition to copyright violations, the unauthorized reproduction and use of this product to benefit a second party may be considered the unauthorized practice of law.

This product is designed to provide authoritative and accurate information in regard to the subject matter covered. However, the accuracy of the information is not guaranteed, as laws and regulations may change or be subject to differing interpretations. Consequently, you may be responsible for following alternative procedures, or using material or forms different from those supplied with this product. It is strongly advised that you examine the laws of your state before acting upon any of the material contained in this product.

As with any matter, common sense should determine whether you need the assistance of an attorney. We urge you to consult with an attorney, qualified estate planner, or tax professional, or to seek any other relevant expert advice whenever substantial sums of money are involved, you doubt the suitability of the product you have purchased, or if there is anything about the product that you do not understand including its adequacy to protect you. Even if you are completely satisfied with this product, we encourage you to have your attorney review it.

Neither the author, publisher, distributor nor retailer are engaged in rendering legal, accounting or other professional services. Accordingly, the publisher, author, distributor and retailer shall have neither liability nor responsibility to any party for any loss or damage caused or alleged to be caused by the use of this product.

Copyright Notice

The purchaser of this guide is hereby authorized to reproduce in any form or by any means, electronic or mechanical, including photocopying, all forms and documents contained in this guide, provided it is for non-profit, educational or private use. Such reproduction requires no further permission from the publisher and/or payment of any permission fee.

The reproduction of any form or document in any other publication intended for sale is prohibited without the written permission of the publisher. Publication for nonprofit use should provide proper attribution to Made E-Z Products™.

Table of contents

Introduction to MLM Made E-Z™

Multi-level marketing (MLM) companies abound. Many economists predict that this type of selling will become *the* preferred method of selling. A lot of people have joined MLM programs and made a fortune from their efforts. Anybody with a smattering of ambition and a dose of energy can still join and attain financial freedom. However, unless you know what you're doing and discover how to do it, you'll probably never succeed.

Be sure the MLM company you choose is all it claims to be— that it will make regular payments to you, ship the merchandise to your customers, and is going to be around for years to come.

Be sure that the product you're promoting has mass appeal— does it sell itself and will people stand in line to buy it? A lot of well-meaning advertising writers advise you to select a product, devise a selling plan and then work on your plan. But, this only turns you into an "Eight-Day-A-Week Sales Person." The one product that sells itself, and for which people the world over will stand in line for is *how-to information* that explains how to get rich.

Finally, make sure the program you decide upon can be adapted to sales by mail, which is the least expensive and most efficient method of selling.

Look at all the ads trying to sell multi-level programs in the trade papers and magazines. What are they missing? Can you adapt your program to "have to have" advertising? This book will tell you how and help you to earn big profits from MLM!

The bare-
bone basics
of MLM

1

Chapter 1

The bare-bone basics of MLM

What you'll find in this chapter:

- ⟶ The basics of multi-level marketing
- ⟶ How to work a multi-level program
- ⟶ Hints to build your organization
- ⟶ MLM programs to watch out for
- ⟶ How to find a program that's right for you

Just what are all those thousands of programs and solicitations spreading a swath across the country called *Multi-Level Marketing (MLM)*? good portion of them are nothing but chain or pyramid schemes, some completely illegal.

> **note**
> The downline is usually set up at three to five levels deep although it seldom gets that far, especially if it is a multi-level program being circulated through the mail.

DEFINITION

A true *multi-level plan* is one in which there is an agreement between yourself and a manufacturer or distributor to purchase products at wholesale and sell them at retail, also with the right to sponsor others (your *downline*) thus multiplying your sales base and profits by receiving a percent of the sales made through your downline. Persons you sponsor show others the program and sign them up as members under themselves. In effect, you multiply your efforts by selling the product through a network of distributors.

A small initial investment is all that is usually required to become a distributor. You should have a flexible schedule but little experience is necessary. For you and your distributors to have any kind of success, you must handle high quality items which can be sold at substantially below retail store prices.

Distributors are charged for the program packet which includes instructions, literature, samples, etc. To be legal, the investment must be only a nominal amount. Sale or consumption of the product must be the prime objective and no fees should be collected for recruiting endeavors.

note

A common problem in recruiting people is getting them to "look at the plan." If they have seen multi-level plans before they won't give anyone a chance to explain as they think they already know all about it. Some get around this by inserting an ad in the local paper, asking interested parties to call about "a good money-making plan." They use a telephone answering machine which advises the caller where and when to attend an "Income Meeting." The machine doesn't give them a chance to ask questions. If they are interested and not just curiosity seekers, they may show up for the seminar.

note **The meetings and personal contacts that represent strength are missing when the business is conducted by mail.**

Multi-level selling by large party plan firms are often successful because they keep their members productive through a series of coaxing, weekly meetings, phone calls and home visits. This stimulates activity and better results are obtained. These elements are often missing in multi-level mail-order programs. Therefore a good many of the multi-level mail-order programs may not work, especially on a 4 or 5 level downline position, unless properly managed and using some of the same techniques as the large plan firms.

A typical multi-level get-rich scheme: you are offered a book selling plan for $5.00. You are assigned a code number and asked to mail 500 brochures.

When your name reaches the fifth level you are supposed to have collected something like $50,000 in commission for 100,000 books which sold for a total of $500,000. This is based on only 10 orders received by you and 10 orders received by each of your downliners who also mailed 500 brochures.

If only 10 people in the entire United States initially worked this one plan with the same success you are supposed to have, there would be 5,000 brochures out the first level; 50,000 the second; 500,000 the third; 5,000,000 the 4th level, and 50 million in the 5th level. That would amount to some $11,000,000 in postage, with brochures delivered to over one-half of the 90,000,000 mail-order buyers in the U.S.

This type of program will collapse under its own weight. After one level there is usually a complete drop-out.

There are too many ways to make an honest living without telling lies so keep your multi-level plans level!

Most such plans get started because of exorbitant, dishonest claims. Tell the truth in an ad on multi-level marketing and there are very few takers. Change the ad to greatly exaggerated claims, such as *earn $100,000 a year working from the home part time* and the inquiries pour in. The response to this kind of ad doesn't mean that anyone will make any money!

As mentioned, unless the organization you are dealing with offers top quality products at discount prices it is very difficult to make a living with the multi-level marketing concept. A person has to knock on a great number of doors, or send out a massive amount of literature through the mail, in order to find qualified people who are interested in pursuing this kind of activity.

CAUTION

If multi-level programs worked as well as many of them advertise, the nation would be flooded with solicitations for every plan on the books.

Being able to work a multi-level plan on a part-time basis at your leisure, with no pressure from the company as to how much of the product you purchase or the amount of business you must bring in each month, is one of the attractions of this kind of activity, but results are usually negative. It's too easy to forget about the business, sit back in your easy chair, and watch TV.

> *note* You may make 200 calls and show the program 100 times before you get even one member who will take an active part in the program.

After a hard day's work at another job it doesn't take long to forget that you have a part-time multi-level program going.

That phone call or that meeting to show the plan is too easy to put off until "tomorrow." Yes, it takes a certain kind of individual to follow through and they are few and far between.

> ⚠ **CAUTION** Watch Out! If products or services are only mentioned as an after-thought, if at all, you're asking for trouble.

Most multi-level plans state that you can make thousands of dollars by duplicating yourself a few times and having your downline do the same. It never works that way. You are fortunate if a small percent of your downline produces much of anything unless you are able to spend a great deal of time teaching and promoting their business as well as your own.

How are you supposed to get prospects and members? Most of the promotional materials suggest you solicit your friends, neighbors and relatives, at least as a starter. Many people are reluctant to "take advantage" of their friends. Of course, if you have the best bargains available "anywhere," you may be doing them a great favor.

Phone calls, word of mouth, direct mail pieces and follow-up, and local classified ads are other methods used to get members and sell the products.

Multi-level companies usually offer newsletters, catalogs, direct mail pieces, and camera-ready material which members can have copied or printed locally. They often have name lists available or advise members how to compile their own lists.

 Mail-order multi-level organizations will usually drop-ship direct to your customers, if you wish. They are also set up to do most of the paperwork and accounting, leaving members with little detail work.

If you decide to try a multi-level program you are usually required to pay a fee, for which you will obtain all the materials and information pertaining to the organization and the products. You may also be asked to purchase some of the items you will be selling. You will contact friends and neighbors, explaining how the program works, try to sell them merchandise from the catalogs and sign them up as members if possible. You will compile lists of prospects and make direct mailings. As your business develops you need to contact those in your downline periodically and offer sympathy, help and assistance in order to make the business grow.

Many other incentives, prizes and extra commissions are offered by some firms.

note You should like people. It's hard to be a good salesman if you don't; and that's what you have to be—a good salesman!

Make sure the organization you choose and the programs they offer are legal. If it is just a pyramid scheme whereby members are merely signing up others for a fee and little if any merchandise is being sold it could be illegal. In any event, this type of operation will produce little if any money-making opportunity.

 Remember also, there are some very fine multi-level firms offering good opportunities for success oriented people. Those who thoroughly enjoy meeting and working with others, who are not afraid of hard work, not easily discouraged and who can persevere in the face of many disappointments, have made their fortunes in multi-level marketing. With such attributes and the right program—together with proper training—you can be a success in this kind of business.

> **note** If in doubt, it is advisable to check out the firm with the Better Business Bureau or with the postal authorities when it involves direct mail methods.

Before you can appreciate and understand how to promote MLM programs by mail, it is appropriate to review first the fundamentals of MLM and proven mail-order methods. Let's talk first about MLM which is also known as networking or network marketing.

The basics of MLM programs

First understand that MLM is not an illegal pyramid scheme. It is 100% legal and many multimillion dollar companies market their product strictly through MLM promotion. Some of the best known MLM companies include Amway, Shaklee, Tupperware, Princess House, a subsidiary of Colgate Palmolive, A.L. Williams, Mary Kay Cosmetics, U.S. Sprint, MCI, and NSA. These companies have been around for decades. There are actually thousands more MLM companies.

> **note** Like other companies, some MLMs are good and some are not so good. But one thing is for sure. MLM is here to stay, and it is an explosive growth field!

So what's the big attraction to MLM companies and programs? Well, it represents a wonderful opportunity for the "little fella" to start his own business on a part time basis and make a whole lot of money! How is this possible? The concept is fairly simple: MLM companies offer their products and services through independent distributors who can then recruit other distributors. That way, a distributor can buy the MLM products at a discount and earn money selling the product directly to others. He also earns

DEFINITION

"overrides" for the distributor that he has sponsored. And, it gets better. Normally, a distributor also earns "overrides" for several levels that are deep in his organization. These distributors are called his *downline* or his *organization.* You have probably seen how an organization can grow, but I'll show you again just in case. Let's say that your organization has 5 levels. Let's assume that you sponsor 5 people, and everyone does likewise. Your downline would then grow like this:

Level	1	5	Distributors
Level	2	25	Distributors
Level	3	124	Distributors
Level	4	625	Distributors
Level	5	3,125	Distributors
Total =		3,905	Distributors

Now that's quite a few distributors. If you earned $10 a month for each distributor in your "downline," you would be earning $39,050 a month! So theoretically, you can earn a lot of money! If everything worked perfectly. But it normally doesn't since your downline will not build perfectly.

In fact, in most cases, if you use standard MLM techniques, you'll be lucky to build anyone on your second level. You can make a lot of money in MLM, but most people don't. You need to understand the underlying principles of MLM first.

You must build your organization deep

Notice in the previous table that you earn your big money on your 5th level. That's because that's where most of your distributors are. To build a deep organization, you must train and help your first level! In other words, you must have a method that is *duplicative.* Your first level people must have a way to help their first level (your 2nd level) and so on. Otherwise, your organization will die on the vine!

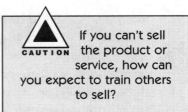

If you can't sell the product or service, how can you expect to train others to sell?

Most new people in MLM make the serious mistake of trying to build their first level wide. That is, they personally want to recruit as many people as they can. Here is how one might reason: If he can't or doesn't want to sell, surely if he sponsors enough people on his first level, some of these people will magically sell for him. Bad mistake. You need a duplicative method that you, your people, and their people can easily copy. This is the fundamental basic rule that makes MLM promoters wealthy! Violate it and you're dead in the water!

You must learn how to sell and teach others to sell

This is the kiss of death for most people! Let's face it, most people hate to sell, can't sell, and don't want to learn how to sell. But, understand that if you are strictly in MLM only, you "gotta" sell. There is no other choice.

note Lead generation is generally very awkward. Since the very principle of MLM is that all selling is done by word of mouth, advertising just doesn't seem to fit.

Another unique problem with MLM'ers is that they find it difficult to generate leads. That is, once you join an MLM company, to whom do you sell? Where do you find interested people to talk to? If advertising is used, it is mostly used nationally, and the long distance phone calls for following up get to be very expensive, quickly. Generally, if your upline gives you a few leads a month, you're lucky. Or, sometimes you will be invited to participate in cooperative advertising. This is OK, but these leads generally cost $1 to $5 each and then again you have the long distance problem.

Oh yes, the MLM companies come up with all kinds of disguised ways to overcome the selling and lead generation problems. They try to teach you how to "share" your product with friends and relatives. They want you to bring your potential distributors to rah, rah, rah "opportunity meetings." All selling techniques. And yes, they show you how you can lose a lot of money by trying to sponsor new distributors by "long distance."

> **note** Can you imagine K-Mart or drug stores if they handled only one brand of products?

Another theory that MLM companies will tout is that you should be 100% loyal to only them. That is, they insist that you are active only with their MLM company. This goes against human nature. Most MLM'ers get into several MLM companies. So this is a contradiction in the minds of most MLM'ers. They want to handle several companies, and most people want to "buy into" several companies, but no MLM company openly discusses it. Certainly no MLM company trains you how to do it.

Illegal multi-level plans

In certain states, some multi-level sales plans are illegal since it is unlawful to organize a pyramid club, or to induce or attempt to induce membership in one.

DEFINITION In such states, a *pyramid club* is a sales device where a person, upon condition of making an investment, is granted a license or right to solicit or recruit for economic gain one or more additional persons who are also granted such license or right upon condition of making an investment, and further perpetrate the chain of

> **note** Pyramid clubs also include any such sales device which does not involve the sale or distribution of any real estate, goods or services, including but not limited to a chain letter scheme. .

persons who are granted such license or right upon such condition.

Pyramids are illegal because they are inherently fraudulent. In order to achieve the profits that are promised, a never ending chain of participants must be recruited. A saturation point is reached and no more recruits are available. When this occurs the most recent recruits can't receive what was held out to them to cause them to join, and they lose all or part of what they paid to join the scheme. After just a few levels there would have to be millions or billions of participants to keep the chain going.

Chain letters are not the only illegal pyramids. As noted, multi-level sales schemes can be illegal also. Many are nothing but chain letter schemes with the nominal addition of some goods or services to be distributed. A pyramid club is present if participants make investments in return for the right to recruit, for economic gain, others who in turn recruit additional participants.

> **note** Legal multi-level marketing systems are designed to distribute goods and services and are not disguised as endless chains.

Both the "investment" and "recruiting" elements must be present to constitute an illegal pyramid scheme. *Recruiting for economic gain* means if anything is received directly or indirectly as a result of recruiting new participants. Even earnings based on sales made by new participants recruited constitutes economic gain.

Evaluating multi-level sales schemes is a difficult process and many considerations must be answered in order to determine the legality or illegality of each program. Is there more stress toward recruitment than for the sale of the product? Are the claims, as to what the earnings are, based on actual experience of typical participants? (They better watch out for the entries made in the IRS computers pertaining to their fabulous income claims.)

Are there misleading representations? You would have to get your attorney to review specific circumstances of each plan or program in order to determine which ones are legal or illegal. Even then, you can't be sure.

Here are a few quick tests that should help you decide. If the MLM offer you're considering can't give believable answers to these crucial questions tell the promoter to take a hike!

- Does the sales literature contain detailed descriptions of its products or services, or only countless references to how easily and quickly you can make money with little work or commitment?

- Does the MLM offer products or services that the public needs and wants?

  This is a trick question. Think about it. Is there really a demand for what you're going to offer? Lots of luck if you get stuck with something that doesn't generate repeat business. It's the lifeblood necessary to generate the commissions you got into the plan for in the first place!

- Can similar products be found in retail stores, or be obtained through mail-order at about the same price? Your commissions and bonuses, if any, are based on sponsoring people who can fill orders. When you have a good product—that's what makes the money for you. If it can be purchased through regular retail channels, ask yourself why people are going to buy from you instead.

- Can you generate repeat sales? If the company has a reputation for quality products you should be able to generate repeat business, build and hold your downline. That's what's necessary for any successful MLM plan.

Have you decided that MLM plan you're thinking about seems to be on the level? Here's what you need to be successful:

- ✦ A quality product or service.

- ✦ A successful attitude. You must live, think, talk, dream success. All day—every day. No exceptions. Sell. Sell. Sell.

+ Believe in yourself, and the company you're working for.

+ Discipline. You will never be successful if you only work at it when you feel like it. Go back and read item # 2 again.

+ Find prospects. If you don't know how, you will never get past first base!

+ Close the sale. You can have the best product, an eager customer with money to spend, but if you can't ask for and get that order, the best sales presentation in the world won't do you any good. To be successful in MLM you must be a really good salesman.

+ You need repeat sales.

+ Recruit new distributors and/or dealers.

Have a realistic goal. Don't aim too high, but you do have to motivate yourself.

A few words on MLM projections and money-back guarantees

One of the best ways to spot a potential phony is a promise of a sizable "guarantee" if you don't at least make $100,000 or some other arbitrary high figure with their program in your first year. Honest companies can't possibly make such an offer, or are not giving you the whole story!

Read the fine print. To collect on the guarantee, you probably have to fulfill a few little requirements—like paying a year's worth of monthly dues, or providing proof you distributed 25,000 brochures, or having at least 10 people in your downline.

Some other things to look for:

- A company with a proven track record in business for at least several years. MLM companies have a strange habit of folding up their tent with little or no warning. Don't get stuck holding the bag.

- Diverse product line. NO door to door selling. That's a big hurdle. If the product can be sold through a simple ad or catalog, it's a lot less wear and tear on you, and burn-out is slower.

- Initial small investment. Don't tie up big bucks buying sample kits and products.

- Proven earnings potential. Talk to several successful members already doing the program. Can't find any? Then how good is the program? If you find many, then how are you going to cut into their action? MLM is a cutthroat, fiercely competitive business!

What you need to know about MLM

2

Chapter 2
What you need to know about MLM

What you'll find in this chapter:

- ➤ History of MLM
- ➤ What you can expect to earn
- ➤ The ultimate test of an MLM company
- ➤ The hardest part of working MLM
- ➤ How to make MLM easier to work

Multi-level marketing is one of the biggest growth industries of business today. It is the industry that made corporate giants of Amway, Shaklee, Mary Kay and Herbalife. It has been termed as the last true rags-to-riches opportunity left in North America, and its ability to bring enormous incomes to almost anyone is legend. In fact, it is expected to create more new millionaires than any other industry, and soon will be the single most popular method of bringing new products to the consumer.

MLM offers an opportunity for anyone to operate their own business. For less than $50 in many cases, you can get involved with a legitimate MLM program and earn from $100 a month to hundreds of thousands of dollars a year. Most incomes fall between those two extremes, but the earning potential of almost any good company is virtually unlimited. The only limits are set by the marketer—their time, energy, persistence, faith in their product, and the people working with them. A superstarter in MLM must be a caring, sharing person, energetic and highly motivated. Some of the most amazing success stories in MLM have been hard-luck Harrys and bored housewives with no previous marketing or sales experience.

The root of MLM success is the sponsoring of new people into their businesses, much in the same way sales agents find new retailers to handle their products. Successful organizations such as Amway and Mary Kay have thousands of distributors, but even these had to start with one or two motivated people sponsoring a few other motivated people.

note The ultimate test of an MLM company is the quality, price and reusability of the product. A good firm is usually founded on products with rapidly expanding popularity, day-to-day use in the home, and a regular repurchase required. They should be better quality and at least as competitively priced as the same goods bought in stores.

note The first multi-level companies sprang up in the 1930's, but they were dinosaurs compared to modern marketing strategies. It wasn't until the mid-60's that MLM gained international prominence.

Multi-level marketing is really a partnership. You go into business with someone who has the same interests and goals as you. You make a commitment to each other. You work with the same people. Working multi-level marketing correctly not only makes success easier, it eliminates many problems.

The hardest thing is to find the person you want to work with (your sponsor). You want someone who is willing to work and assist you when needed. You should join programs under the same person all the time. This makes for a solid downline. If your sponsor isn't interested in a particular program, contact his sponsor. By doing this, you strengthen your group.

Many people complain about others stealing their people. They seem to think that just because they signed someone up once, they should always have them. If someone gives their downline the help and assistance they should, there would be no need for them to worry about someone stealing them away. They should want to continue with you because they know you will help them. Why should someone stick with you if all you do is collect commissions from them? Can you really blame them for not following you into other programs?

Take a look at the other side of the "coin." Having the right people in your downline is just as important as having the right sponsor. If someone sponsored you into a program and helped you, don't expect them to sign you into another program if you haven't tried to do anything on your own. Granted, they make money for those they sponsor for you, but why should they make you money if you don't do anything?

 Mailing out hundreds of brochures may get you several people in your downline. This may look good on a printout, but what about on a commission check? Would you rather have a printout a foot long with a small check—or a small printout with a large check?

 Be choosy about whom you recruit. Let them know what you expect from them and what they can expect from you. Level with them completely about the program you are trying to get them into. Having 2 or 3 good people will make you more money than having 10 or 12 deadbeats.

Don't join every program that comes along. Find one you like and work it. It takes time to build a solid downline. Help your downline and have them do the same. This way everybody will make money.

Be careful what you promise people. Remember, nothing is guaranteed. Be as honest as you can. Don't tell someone you'll do something if you can't.

> **note** You can't expect to keep your downline if you leave them stranded when you become profitable. You have to help them profit too. They will be more apt to follow you in other programs this way.

Offer your help, but guarantee nothing. No matter how good something might seem, it might not work. If you mislead people, how long do you expect to keep them?

Doing things this way may take a little longer, but look at the advantages!

- You have a solid downline.

- You don't have to race to the phone or mailbox to be first to contact someone.

- Because you are working with the same people, you will get to know them.

- You will have a steady income. You don't have to worry about finding new "schemes" and new "victims" every few months.

note

Actually, four things are needed to be successful in MLM: A good product, a good marketing structure, a good sponsor and a strong downline. The time and money spent to find these four things are well worth it. Don't settle for anything less. To do so will only restrict the goals you can achieve.

Once you have found these four things, it's easy. All you have to do is keep in touch with your 5 or 6 people. If everyone does this, no one will fail. Everybody will be a success.

Here are the barebones mechanics of MLM:

- ✦ You become involved with an MLM company first as a customer because the product offers substantial quality and savings.

- ✦ Because the products are good, you tell others about them.

- ✦ Rather than send these people to your distributors, you become a sponsored distributor yourself for these new people. And, if these people (let's say there are five) each knows five others who will buy the product, you have 25 people buying products through you.

+ If these 25 each know five people, you have 125. If those 125 know five people, you have 625 at the fourth level buying through you in a distributor's network you built from only five people. If these people purchased only $30 worth of products a month, that would be $300,000 in gross sales, and you could expect to earn at least one quarter of that figure, probably much more.

> **E-Z TIP**
>
> Choose your product line carefully, recruit heavily and always expand your business education as you grow. MLM is a big field with big rewards for absolutely anyone who can commit themselves to success at any cost.

+ Commission and bonuses vary with product and company, but most go through four to eight levels, and have two or three levels at which substantial higher commissions are paid. This encourages new distributors to build those levels.

+ Some of the networks-inside-of-the-networks will end at certain levels with people buying but not sponsoring new people. And some will involve more than five people. Distributors will always be your best customers and biggest moneymakers.

+ The best companies are the blue chip firms offering a wide range of products such as Amway and Shaklee. New ones emerge all the time and some of the more faddish MLM companies die quickly. But, they can still make good money quickly for distributors with established downlines.

How to pick a winning MLM plan

3

Chapter 3

How to pick a winning MLM plan

What you'll find in this chapter:

➠ Questions to ask about MLM programs

➠ How to set your own personal MLM goals

➠ Programs you should avoid

➠ The pitfalls of chain letters

➠ The pitfalls of pyramid schemes

The idea of using a multi-level marketing program to produce extra income—to attain total financial freedom—has taken the world by storm! More and more people attempt to find a real winner every year.

The problem is that multi-level marketing companies are sprouting up all over the place, and there are just too many for the average extra-income opportunity seeker. This makes the choice of the best ones a frustrating and time-consuming process.

Before you "hook up" with any company, consider the product and the operation:

- Think about the product. Is it a product that you would use regularly, and freely recommend to your friends? Is it lower-priced, more convenient to use than similar products available elsewhere, particularly at the stores in your area. What about delivery? How much of a time interval is involved from when your customer orders until he receives the product?

- Find out as much about the operation as you possibly can. Beware of chain letters, pyramid scams, and exorbitant claims relative to distributor profits. Be sure to find out exactly what you'll get in return for your initial sign-up fee. Make sure the company provides you with professional sales aid materials, and that they're reasonably priced—many MLM companies rake in tremendous profits just selling brochures and/or other sales literature—check with your local printing outlets and determine your actual cost.

In essence, before deciding to become involved in a multi-level marketing company and expecting to make a profit, it is essential that you understand:

- It is a selling proposition—you will be required to do at least some face-to-face selling—and it will require a lot of your time.

- You must have a product line that appeals to most people—in other words, information or program/help that enables people to fulfill their basic wants. Selling vitamins, wrinkle creams, even food, will NOT fulfill those needs because of the intense competition. But, appealing to those people who are already selling a product with a sales improvement or training program can make you rich.

> **E-Z TIP**
>
> Find out about the company's financial backing and corporate officers. Are they in it as full-time professional sales people? Be sure to understand how the company keeps track of all the incoming orders, and when and how you will be paid.

In addition to understanding what's involved, and having a product line that most people want and will purchase from you, you need assistance and instructions—in not only selling the product or products, but in how to find new customers on an ongoing basis. Once you decide to try your hand at multi-level marketing, the next thing is to determine how YOU want to sell it—will you be selling door-to-door, via home parties, public seminars, by mail, or a combination of all these methods?

Remember, the amount of time you spend in actually trying to sell the product will determine the amount of money you make. The more presentations or sales calls you make, the more money you're going to make—but unless you make those sales calls, you won't be making any money.

Your best defense against getting involved in illegal schemes and the "LOSERS," is knowing what to look for, thereby knowing what to avoid. These important guidelines enhance the chances of picking the "BIG WINNERS" in MLM. You too, may now use this as a check list before making any final decision:

+ **Avoid the many "get rich quick" offers** like "Earn $100,000 Over the Weekend," or something like that. Legitimate multi-level businesses and consultants are at the heart of a vast communications network and have never . . . repeat NEVER . . . heard of anybody earning vast amounts of money with such offers.

> *note*
> It's up to you to decide just how much time you'll spend with your extra-income producing project.

+ **Avoid chain letters.** Marketing products through the MLM concept is one thing, a "chain letter" is another. Even if the chain letter has a product such as a report, it is still considered a chain letter by Postal Authorities and may get you the wrong kind of attention. Some even say "this one is LEGAL . . . Refer to Postal Statute No.XXXX." DON'T BUY IT! A "chain letter" is a chain letter

PERIOD. If you must send the name or names on the letter a sum of money and add your name, expecting others to send you money, you will be involved in a chain letter.

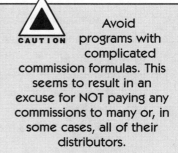
Avoid programs with complicated commission formulas. This seems to result in an excuse for NOT paying any commissions to many or, in some cases, all of their distributors.

✦ **Avoid pyramid schemes.** Many people do not know the difference between a pyramid plan and a merchandise based marketing plan. You can spot a pyramid plan:

- They offer rewards for the act of recruiting.

- Large inventory purchases are required to join their programs.

- They lack interest in retailing to the consumer and they make deceptive claims designed to defraud people of money. Legitimate MLM companies require new distributors to purchase only one or a few items of what they want and the product is probably one they would buy anyway.

✦ **Avoid plans with more than seven levels.** Firms using more than 7 levels do so to make the profits look fantastic at the last few levels. These are usually the ones that pay low commissions and offer products that are overpriced.

✦ **Avoid programs offering to print and mail brochures for you.** There is NO WAY for you to know how many will actually be mailed. Also, if any are mailed, it is usually done by "Bulk Rate" which is the most ineffective way to send them out .

✦ **Avoid plans promoting products not useful to most people, or that cost more than the retail price paid in stores.** Also beware of any plan that lets people become distributors without buying a product. This is not fair because most distributors, when given this option, will not buy the product. This results in lost sales all the way down the line.

Now that you know what to avoid, you are better equipped and ready to select a genuine MLM opportunity of your liking.

How to establish a profitable downline

4

Chapter 4

How to establish a profitable downline

What you'll find in this chapter:

➠ Why you need an instruction sheet

➠ How to work well with your dealers

➠ What to do with someone who doesn't work

➠ Developing word-of-mouth sales

➠ What a circular can do for the MLM program

Do you give your customers enough information to work your program?

While the originator of the program knows exactly what to do, most of your customers do not. What may seem like common sense to you is not as understandable to others who purchase it.

Every program you sell should come with an instruction sheet, just like any product you purchase. It just makes good business sense to include an instruction sheet or booklet with anything you sell.

Guess what? This sheet or booklet can be used to YOUR advantage. By explaining step-by-step how the program works, what its goals are, the benefits of working it and what steps to take in order to work it properly, you can offer different options to help your customer. If you supply camera-ready circulars, you could offer to print copies, supply pre-printed envelopes and

DEFINITION
mailing list names for an additional price. This is called *back-end sales.*

And, if you don't provide these items, you can find a wide range of mail order dealers who can. Hook up with a good supplier who will reduce their prices slightly so you can make a profit and send orders directly to them from your "back-end" sales. This little bit of extra money is what helps your program become more financially solid.

 So many programs fail because they are not managed and structured properly. Remember the old saying: "A 3-legged stool is not easily broken?" It's true. The more "branches" you have in a program that generates some cash flow the better. DON'T get this confused with nickel-and-diming people to death. Just give them the product they pay for and offer them extra products they can purchase that complement what they already have.

One of the biggest mistakes you can make when you are the Prime Source of any program is to promote the program your dealers are also promoting. Instead of it bringing in more money it has the opposite effect—it destroys the program!

> **note** It's only good business sense to help your dealers by providing them with tips and information to work your program.

Let's say that Melanie joins Jeff's program. Jeff is the Prime Source and provides Melanie with a camera-ready circular with her name on it. Melanie begins printing and mailing the circular in her own mailings but one day she spots Jeff advertising his own circular in a tabloid. What does Melanie do? She STOPS mailing her circular. Why? Because Jeff looks like a greedy dealer who is after all the profit. Jeff is only giving Melanie 50% when people respond to her circular and Jeff gets 100% if people respond to his circular. Also, Melanie does not want to be in competition with Jeff and drops out of the program. It's not fair to Melanie.

What happens to Jeff's potential income when all his dealers see the circulars with his name on them? You got it. They all drop out. Now what happens to Jeff's income? It drops considerably!

Instead, Jeff should select a few of his dealers who are trying their best to make money with his program and offer to mail pre-printed circulars for them free of charge. Remember that Jeff is making money from every sale generated by his dealers, so by promoting his own product he is still making money. Besides, if he helps his dealers make a few dollars, what will his dealers do? They will keep participating in Jeff's program and most of them will re-invest the commission money they make into printing and mailing more circulars.

> **note** Sure, there will always be people who buy into your programs and not work them, but you'll lose a lot more money if you step on their toes and become their competition! Be wise!

Also, when they begin to make a little money, they will tell everybody they know what a wonderful program Jeff has. Guess what? Jeff will get more dealers promoting his program which means more money for Jeff in the long run. Jeff's a success because he made his dealers a success.

Finally, Jeff's reputation will escalate because all his dealers will know he's an honest guy to do business with. Guess what? Jeff's business income increases! Not just because of the program but because people are interested in other things Jeff sells.

Guaranteed ways to keep your downline active and buying

5

Chapter 5

Guaranteed ways to keep your downline active and buying

What you'll find in this chapter:

➠ Why you need to build your program deep

➠ How to build a deep MLM organization

➠ How to keep your downline motivated

➠ Which advertising works the best

➠ Managing finances

Master these concepts and it is time for you and your downline to celebrate.

As you become more familiar with MLM, you will eventually reach a very important conclusion: You want to build your MLM organization DEEP! But, let's review this just in case it is not crystal clear in your mind. It is so important for you to understand this principle. The very backbone of your success with a MLM program is that you are able to multiply your efforts through others. That way, your organization multiplies such that your 3rd, 4th 5th and so on levels attain a large number of people in your organization—or downline.

You will always earn the large money in your deep levels. In fact, a lot of MLM programs are geared so you make more on your deep levels (per person) than what you will earn on your first level. For example, if you were to recruit

1,000 members on your first level, you earn about $3,000 per month. Conversely, if these same 1,000 people were on your 3rd level, you would earn about $23,000 a month. That's a big difference. So you see there are two very important reasons to build your downline deep. First, that is where the large number of people will be. The second reason is that many MLM programs pay much more per person in your deep levels.

The "Secret Key" to building a deep organization is fairly simple. You must help your first level, and then teach them how to help *their* first level! In other words, you must have a system that is 100% duplicative. To do this, you must first have a method that works for you. You then show your first level how to replicate your method. Last, but most important, you must be able to teach your first level to teach their first level! To look at this another way, you must be able to HELP your first level and show them how to help their first level of downline.

> **note** If I can help you, and we both make money, then I am motivated to help you. Right? That's how MLM works. When it's done properly, MLM is a beautiful system. You don't have to sell the world. Only a few in your first level.

If you want to build a large MLM organization, you do so by primarily working with your first level of people. Agree? Just imagine. Let's say you start with 10 people. If your MLM program has 5 levels, it can grow 10 x 10 x 10 x 10 x 10 = 100,000 on your 5th level! Now admittedly, that is a perfect mathematical model, and it is unlikely that will happen and we both know it. But, if you have a good system that really can be implemented, you probably can get close! Let's talk a little more about how many people you should sponsor on your first level. You decide, but you should use this as a guideline: "Sponsor only those that you can help." In this program, *help* is more or less defined as your capability to generate leads and make some mailings for your first level of downline. In other words, if you follow the techniques in this guide, you will be able to generate many good qualified leads that you will want to pass (sell) on to your downline. If

DEFINITION

you have some upfront cash to advertise or whatever, you may be able to help more than 10 people. On the other hand, if you are truly starting on a shoestring, maybe you can help only a few. But, you decide. The objective is simple. Decide how many ACTIVE people you want on your first level, and then go for it!

You will no doubt sign up people who will not do anything! When that happens, don't be discouraged. Instead, you need to find a replacement who will be active. If you set your goal to have 10 active people in your first level, don't stop until you meet your goals. Remember, as soon as you sign up one or two people in your first level, you will want to help these people as well as filling out your own first level. During this period, your upline is available to help you. Therefore, your upline is helping you, you are helping yourself, and you are helping your downline—all at the same time. Take this into consideration before you commit to how many people you want to build in your first level. You also should set a goal in your mind for how long it will take you to fill in your first level. Rome was not built in a day, so give yourself enough time. The important thing is to stick to it. If you stay with it long enough, it will blossom out for you.

note

> **E-Z TIP**
>
> Make sure you "lean" on your upline sponsor, and you in return provide assistance to your downline. We all help each other to make this work for all of us.

Lastly, keep your troops motivated! This strategy will work for you and your downline. It takes some time and effort on everyone's part! Anything worthwhile seldom comes totally free. If you follow the steps in this guide, your chances of success are very high. It is really quite simple. If you make money quickly, you will be motivated to work your program. So will the people that you sign up.

Now, how do you keep you and your people happy and motivated? There are a few basic rules you need to know and adopt.

✦ Promote forced payment MLM plans.

There are all kinds of MLM programs. In many, you can join and stay active by just paying yearly organizational fees. Participate in MLM programs in which everyone is more or less forced to buy something every month. That way, you are more or less guaranteed that all members in your downline contribute to your income. For example, I know some people that have over 1,000 people in their organization, but no one is buying anything! No one is making money! Just wasting it on recruiting new members. That doesn't make any sense. I realize that it is tougher to recruit people into a program that requires you to pay, say $50 a month. Then again, you don't have to recruit the world! Only ten will do very nicely.

✦ Teach your first level to concentrate on local promotion.

The quickest way to promote MLM programs is locally. Why? Because you can circulate postcards and mini-flyers immediately. You can place ads in local newspapers that will be circulated within the week. You want your first level of people to get instant gratification. No waiting. Get them started immediately so they can taste sweet success immediately. There is nothing quite like getting money in your mail box to build confidence.

In local areas, it is a good bet that few people, if any, have seen the postcard offer. And, there are millions of people! This is how the thin edge of MLM and mail-order merge together very subtly. Remember, you should try to sign up only 10 or so people in your first level. In you own "Warm Inner Circle" and in your own neighborhood, you must have 10 people who you can sign up. Circulate the postcards and mini-flyers. It's easy, fast and inexpensive.

note True, national advertising is excellent and you may be tempted to become active in this right away. But, it takes time and you have the risk of increased competition.

✦ Encourage them to participate in several mail-order programs.

The more mail-order programs you and your downline participate in, the more money you both will earn. The stronger you become financially, the better to carry on and help your downline. Buy and resell as many reprintable reports as you can afford, and "buy into" some of the mail-order distributorships that you can resell. You can then expand again.

✦ Encourage your downline members to participate in two or three MLM programs at the same time.

We talk a lot about diversification, but there are some of the benefits for you and your downline. By using different companies to promote your MLM company, your efforts can be multiplied if you offer more than one MLM company. This is only true if you have a coherent plan to market more than one MLM program at the same time. Therefore, if you can afford to handle two or three MLM companies, you maximize your profits for just about the same effort.

✦ Sell your MLM leads to your first level.

This is your first responsibility to your first level. It is the most important thing to teach your people to do for their people. It is not that hard to do, and you make money doing it. This concept is so important that an entire book was written on the subject, *How to Build Your Downline Deep by Selling Leads . . . and Literature.* Here is a summary:

> *note*
> Do not become an "MLM junkie" just to have several companies. If your MLM companies complement each other, you have a chance to multiply your earnings.

If you used any of the promotional methods described in this program, you can surely generate more leads than what you need in order to sign up your first level of 10 active people. When that happens, it is time for you to concentrate on helping and teaching your new people. The fastest and best way to do this is to simply offer the surplus leads that you have generated to your newly recruited people.

Let's review how these extra leads might be generated. If you studied the complete set of reports, you will find many promotional ways that you probably are using. Perhaps you circulated the mini-flyers, sent a few postcards to your "Warm Inner Circle," and maybe you placed some classified ads or small space ads nationally. Before you know it, you sold a few report packages, and you built your first level of distributors. But the reports keep getting copied and recopied. With it, the request to send literature out (with payments) keep coming . . . and coming!

You are in a perfect position to really help your downline and build a deep organization. Remember, people are paying you to send to them your sales literature, and you can sell these leads to your downline. But, don't get greedy. Remember our example program in which you could earn $27.00 for each person that you personally recruit? Stop and think now!

> **CAUTION** Remember, everything that you do must be 100% duplicative, so don't make claims that you can't back up. Don't make claims about things only you can do, and your downline can't do.

In this example, you make your big money on your third level. Instead of recruiting this person for yourself, you simply sell this lead to your downline members for only $1.00! You help your downline members, and you build your third level where the big continuous money is. Everyone wins. Is this duplicative or what? You bet it is.

You find other offers in which the person sends in at least a SASE (Self Addressed Stamped Envelope) with extra cash or stamps. If a person does this, do you think he is anxious to buy? Remember, this person already has the reports, and knows what this program is all about. He sure is interested. Is this a good quality lead? It doesn't get any better.

You now have a fist full of mail-order type "inquiries." All these inquiries are self addressed stamped envelopes with an extra postage stamp. What is this lead worth? Some of these inquiries want information on reprintable reports, mail-order dealerships and some want information on other programs. For those who want information on the reprintable reports and mail-order dealerships, send them yourself! If you have a new person that is struggling, you might, as a personal favor, sell them a few at $1 each. What the heck? That more than pays for your advertising costs. You should consider handling your leads this way too.

> **note**
>
> What about the leads wanting specific program information? I ALWAYS offer these to my downline at $1 each and also offer to mail the literature for them. That way, they build their downline. That's exactly what I want to happen. You should too!

In some MLM programs, the literature and video tapes are very expensive to send out at your cost. Don't do it! I mean, don't do it at your cost. But, do send the complete package. Here's how:

Let's say you have someone that is interested in your MLM program and the complete package of promotional material of color literature and video tapes, etc. which costs you $20. Instead of sending out everything like they should, some make their own poor copies and then tell the person if they are interested they will send the video. Or, they tell the person to send $10 for the video. How do you think the prospective distributor feels? What does he think? He wonders if this is how he is supposed to sell this wonderful MLM program. Not a good impression.

Instead, be totally up front with these people. Remember that you only need to sign up 10 or so people in your first level, so you can be a little bit "picky." We make no bones about that in our advertisements. For the inexpensive mailings, we ask for only $1.00. For the expensive packages, we simply explain that we want to make sure he gets the complete promotional package, but he has to pay for it for reviewing. If he is not interested, he can return it in good condition, and we'll refund his money less the postage and handling costs. We only ask that we get paid for the postage and handling! That way, you can be assured that your prospective distributor is getting the complete first class package, and you don't lose money sending it to him.

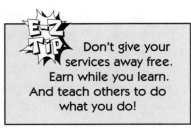
Don't give your
services away free.
Earn while you learn.
And teach others to do
what you do!

This person may instead send off for similar literature from someone else that is sending it free. But, how long do you suppose this person will continue to do this before he realizes he can go broke doing this? How is he supposed to duplicate this method? You can't and don't want to personally sponsor everyone that is possible. Instead, you want 10 good active people. That way, you can be selective. In fact, if the truth were known, the people that you sponsor on your first level will have a tremendous advantage. Isn't this worth quite a bit? If you have a sponsor that is actively promoting this program, he is able to help you immediately with hot, fresh, qualified leads. People that already have these reports. Compare that to sending to one of those "lone souls" that offer free, second-rate literature. You offer a true value to all people that you sponsor. You have a first class program.

✦ Stay in touch with your first level of downline.

After you sign up someone on your first level, stay in touch by letter or phone to make sure they are happy, active and prospering. You want to do this for two reasons. First of all, your lifeline in MLM is to make sure that your first level of people sponsor their fair share of 10 or so active people. If they have trouble, help them out. Feed them leads and offer advice on what worked for you. In other words, share your success methods.

The second reason is that if your first level has by chance become inactive, you must replace them with someone new. If someone becomes inactive, or worse yet, never starts, don't fret. Some people just never will do anything. If that's the case, forget them and replace them. Tough line, but do it! We're only talking about your earnings!

✦ Sell your upline.

If you have other MLM programs, you might have an opportunity to enroll your existing upline members in those programs. What would happen if you go to your "Big Time" upline and explain your programs to them? Just think about this. Do you think they will be in favor of this? Of course! Now, what would happen if you interested them in some of the programs that you are in and they aren't? Do you think you might be able to sign them up to some of your programs? Maybe. And, if you do, how many people do you think they might be able to expose to your new programs? A lot, I bet! Well, it is worth a try. If you can pull this off, you can get an awful lot of people recruited in a big hurry.

> **E-Z TIP**
> Your job is to make sure that you keep a vigorous first level of distributors that do the same as you.

✦ Offer cooperative advertising.

E-Z TIP

Let's say you have 10 strong active people in your first level. Wouldn't it be nice if they collectively advertised together? If each person threw in a few bucks, they could generate a lot of leads for them and their downline. It just takes a little coordination on your part. After all, you know who your first level of people are, and they don't necessarily know each other. It is up to you to make this suggestion to your people and it's easy to do. Why not try? They will probably appreciate your efforts. After all, they stand to earn a lot more money if they do so. But you will have to put it together.

✦ Discreetly help build your first level's downline.

If you become active in this program, you have the opportunity to sign up more people than you need in your first level. It works something like this: All of a sudden you begin to make some serious money. You are generating more extra leads. Your spouse, kids and friends spread the word. You now are approached by all kinds of people who want to "get in this deal." And, oh yes, some of that literature you sent out months ago now starts coming in with people who want to join. Here's your chance to help a few struggling people on your first level.

note If you follow the simple steps in this program, you too could be one of the elite 3% who may earn over $100,000! That wouldn't be too hard to take, would it?

Instead of signing these new people in your first level, have the application sent to you and assign these to a few select people who really need a little help. Now, be careful. You can't be expected to build your first level's organization. But you can help a little when you can.

✦ Encourage your first level to participate in MLM training programs.

Most MLM companies have methods available to help train you to promote their products. If these are available, by all means buy them, attend the seminars and the like. They are generally worth the money and time. Better yet, in some MLM programs, you can earn extra profits when your downline participates in this training program. By all means, take advantage of these fine programs. It will not only help you, but it will help your downline. And, you can earn extra profits. Good deal!

Summary

If you think about what was said in this chapter, it is truly amazing. Most people try to "fight" the basic MLM fundamental truth. Don't try to recruit the whole world. Only a few. That's not really that hard. Not when you use this program. Just imagine. You sell 10 or so report packages and then you recruit only 10 people. They do the same. Really, is that very difficult?

MLM tips, tricks & traps revealed

6

Chapter 6

MLM tips, tricks & traps revealed

Here's a step-by-step procedure for starting, operating and optimizing a mail-order/MLM based business—without making serious mistakes along the way. There are volumes of books on this subject, so this guide will not attempt to "rehash" the "rose colored" views of these authors. Instead, this guide shows you a "lean, mean, cut-to-the-bone" quick and easy way to succeed in your business based upon what the "pros" in the field have done to achieve their incredible incomes. Also, there are tips, useful tricks, and traps to avoid.

Why most people fail in MLM

As explained in other chapters, MLM offers explosive growth opportunity that is surely here to stay. Let's review some MLM facts. There appear to be thousands of MLM companies, but most are not. Many people have become wealthy in MLM, but about 97% of would-be MLM'ers never make it! Therefore, before we go blindly into MLM, let's analyze why 97% of the would-be MLM'ers don't survive. Let's break down the problem into three categories.

1) MLM'ers can't effectively recruit new members.

2) MLM'ers can't keep this program going. It runs out of gas and dies a natural death.

3) MLM Company has serious problems.

I believe that sums it up. Either the MLM'er can't get the program started, can't keep it going, or the MLM company itself goes "belly up."

Why new MLM'ers can't effectively recruit new members

The MLM paradox

DEFINITION

According to Webster, the word *paradox* means, "something with seemingly contradictory qualities or phrases." In MLM, there is a confusing paradox that must be understood and dealt with. Here is the problem. MLM companies by law cannot aggressively "push" the MLM opportunity as the main reason for joining their program. They must emphasize their products and services and explain the MLM opportunity as simply a nice extra benefit. If they don't, all kinds of local, state and federal government officials will attack them. Therefore, they must be extremely careful about what their literature, advertising and promotional material states, what they say in meetings, etc. That is why we normally don't mention an MLM company name when I use examples in these chapters. I do this just to avoid this kind of problem.

All MLM'ers are aware of the MLM paradox problem. Everyone knows, including the MLM companies and all the distributors, that the real reason most people get involved with MLM is for the opportunity. Yet, the MLM literature and the MLM distributor cannot tell you this directly without crossing over the fine line of legality.

> ⚠ **CAUTION** It is illegal to promote an MLM company if the sole purpose is to earn profits by signing up new distributors with no regard to the usefulness of the product or service.

Where does this leave the new MLM distributor? Well, no one is officially allowed to tell him how to go out and aggressively recruit new members. Instead, he is always taught how to "promote" the product and then "as an afterthought" explain the opportunity. All upstanding MLM companies will follow this procedure.

Here are a few helpful methods for resolving the paradox problem:

◆ *TIP:* Keep your lead generating methods separate from your MLM promotions. In other words, it is perfectly legal to promote an opportunity any way you want to as long as you don't tie this directly to an MLM company. That means that you can write your own advertisements, etc. and generate all kinds of leads. When it comes time to discuss a particular MLM company, then use the official MLM literature, guidelines, etc., when presenting that particular company, products, and opportunities. In that way, you make a clear distinction between "lead generating" and promoting a particular "MLM company opportunity."

◆ *TRICK:* Use reports about MLM as your lead generating vehicle. That's the "back bone" purpose of the program . . . to generate MLM leads! Reports do not speak for any particular MLM company. Instead, they provide a method of operating a mail-order "core" business that pays for itself while you automatically generate MLM leads.

◆ *TRAP:* Don't attempt to promote and advertise any particular MLM company's opportunity before you explain the product or service. This is an action that is in direct conflict with the MLM company's guidelines. Instead, find people with a sincere interest in MLM opportunities, and send them the entire official MLM package.

> **E-Z TIP**
> When it comes time to "promote" a particular MLM company, let your customers request literature for the MLM company that interests them. Then use the official MLM literature.

MLM concepts are way too complicated

When most people are exposed to their first MLM opportunity, they may be overpowered by the complexity and newness of MLM concepts and terms. They may become confused by all the new terms such as *Network, Downline, Upline, Organization, Levels,* etc. Then, the specific MLM plan being presented is always anything but simple. There is too much to absorb quickly.

Unfortunately, this generates much suspicion. Is this a pyramid scheme? Is it legal? They probably never heard of the MLM company and that adds to the problem. They find it hard to believe that they can really make the kind of money being discussed. They probably suspect the MLM distributor. And on and on. So what happens? In most cases, nothing—they simply don't sign up! To resolve this, try the following:

◆ *TIP:* Sell reports about MLM first. That way, your potential candidate is educated, and most of the initial education problems are overcome.

◆ *TRICK:* Be selective. Don't try to sell your MLM program to everyone. Instead, spend your time selectively, writing or phoning only those people who already bought the MLM reports.

◆ *TRAP:* If you signed up with an upline person who is *not* promoting your program, you can have a problem. If your upline is also promoting your program, he is in an excellent position to help you.

Potential MLM member can't decide which MLM company to join

Put yourself in your potential MLM member's shoes. If he investigated other MLM companies, he is sure to be confused with all those offers and different companies. If he can't decide, he just doesn't sign up with any MLM company—does he?

There are literally thousands and thousands of MLM distributors who will jump at the chance to tell you which companies you should get into and promote. If you want more "advice," there are many books written by the "experts." Understand one thing. Every book and magazine article that you read and everyone that you talk to will almost assuredly have a "vested interest." In other words, they are either openly or subtly trying to get you to sign up with their program. They will be quick to explain that there are "golden rules" and guidelines to follow. Some will tell you to stay away from "ground floor" opportunities since they are too risky. Others will explain that this is where the big money is. Some will explain why matrix MLM programs are better that others—and visa versa. Some will adamantly advise you to be active in only one MLM company—"be loyal" is their motto. Others try to sign you up for multiple companies. Still others put together "Downline Building Teams," and will invite you to join them. They do all the work (you simply send them money). With all this "good" advice, what is correct?

I noticed one thing about all these "good" advice sources. They never seem to ask what your goals are. What is it that you want? How in the world can someone give another person advice before he understands what the objectives are? How much can you afford to spend? How much risk are you willing to take? What MLM programs and products do you like? Before we even think about selecting a MLM company, let's review the real world about MLM companies and opportunities.

Most new MLM companies never make it through their second year. This is because they are not properly financed, don't really have a good offering, or the federal government shuts them down when unscrupulous people are involved.

note

MLM is no different from other companies, that frankly, have about the same survival length. New companies in any business, MLM or not, have a tough time getting through the first few years.

The people that promote MLM companies never seem to explain the real facts to you. But you need to understand the dark side as well as the "rose colored glasses" view.

note

"How do you select the right MLM company?" This is like asking. "What stock should I buy?" Brokers, advisory firms, and the like will be quick to offer their advice. They all earn fat commissions or other fees. Do you think any of them really care about you? If they really believed in their own "advice," why don't they mortgage their homes and buy-in themselves? The fact is, "No one knows!" That is true with MLM companies and for buying stocks! A standard solution does exist however: Diversify! Spread your investment around. Why put all your eggs into one basket?

All of this doesn't mean that you should select your MLM company(s) blindly. There are fundamental rules and guidelines for you to consider. Once you and your downline are recruited, it is up to the MLM company to provide quality products and services. Here is some advice:

- **Enroll in at least 2 or 3 MLM programs.** This just makes good business sense. As you know, actively and effectively promote all your programs. There is no guarantee that any MLM program will survive, so let's not be naive. Safety is in numbers. Although I chose these companies and have highly recommended a few to the best of my ability, one could go sour. But, they all won't go sour . . . at least not at the same time. In the meantime, you should be making money with the one or two companies that you're in.

- **Build your own core MLM company from one that's at least five years old** and is the best that you can find. Since some of these can be promoted easier and faster, you want to vigorously promote these programs while you are building your slower, but stronger #1 program.

- **Get into MLM companies in which you have total confidence.** There is nothing quite as frustrating as trying to promote a product or a company in which you don't really believe. Stick with those winners having a few years of success behind them.

- **Make sure that the MLM company(s) you select has inexpensive, cost-effective literature** you can send by mail. This just makes good mail-order sense.

Don't be an "MLM junkie" without a plan. Human nature entices you to join many different, exciting "ground floor" MLM opportunities. These can be fine, but you will lose your shirt if you don't have a coherent plan that makes sense. Work this program and its offering to the fullest before you take off in other directions.

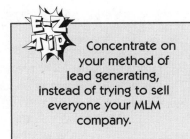

Concentrate on your method of lead generating, instead of trying to sell everyone your MLM company.

No upline support

Once a person joins a new MLM program, he is vulnerable and needs a lot of help from something or someone. In many cases, for whatever reason, his upline is not actively helping him. This happens when the upline person is simply sponsoring too many people with no regard to what happens to them after they get sponsored.

◆ *TIP:* Depend more on your lead generating "system" instead of your upline personnel. Look, we are all human. If I sponsor you, and I die tomorrow, where does that leave you? If you are completely dependent upon my ability to help you, then you would be in big trouble. Stick with some MLM s that require no upline. The you can survive with or without your upline. In that way, any help that you get from your upline is "gravy."

> **EZ TIP** In most standard MLM programs, it is important that the new person get immediate assistance from a local person. Otherwise chances for survival are slim to none.

◆ *TRICK*: Buy some leads from your upline if you need them, and sell surplus ones to your downline.

◆ *TRAP:* Be wary of "downline building" companies. They want to sponsor you, but you could wind up paying as much as $200 for each person they arrange for you to sponsor.

New MLM'ers can't sell

This is probably the major reason most people don't make it in MLM. By using standard MLM techniques, you have to be able to sell. You also must learn how to speak at opportunity meetings.

◆ *TRICK:* Use the mail-order offerings to earn profits while you are promoting MLM opportunities.

◆ *TRAP:* Don't attempt the conventional MLM methods of selling by mail. Since these methods are attempted by thousands of other distributors in the same company, they generally are ineffective and very costly.

MLM'ers cannot generate good leads

Next to the selling problem, this has to be the next biggest reason most people fail in MLM. Let me paint you a picture of what normally happens. The new person just signed up for an exciting MLM program. He is taught by the manuals, meetings and so forth how he should "share" his product with his friends, neighbors and relatives. Normally, he is not comfortable with this, and if he is typical, he will have many sleepless nights, tossing and turning. He just doesn't want to "impose" on his friends! He would feel a lot more comfortable presenting his opportunity to strangers. But to whom? Unless his upline sponsor can get to him immediately, this guy is sure to be a fatality!

◆ *TIP:* Use the mini-flyers to circulate locally and mail postcards to your "inner warm circle." That way you can generate all the leads you want, and you don't have to impose on anyone.

◆ *TRICK:* Explain your program to a few close friends and propose a business venture that you and they will do some local advertising. That way, you can sign up your friends and will generate a lot of fast leads.

◆ *TRAP:* Don't procrastinate! You may have a wonderful opportunity, but if you don't take action, you will be "dead in the water."

MLM'ers sell by mail using standard MLM techniques

To sell by mail, use the report package approach. You can start and operate a profitable mail-order business while generating MLM leads. Run your "core" business like a mail-order business instead of an MLM business. Promote your mail-order business locally first, and then expand it nationally if you like. That way, you keep your up front cost down and you get fast results.

Unless the MLM company has a proven mail-order method (and that's very unlikely), never, never attempt to promote the MLM program by mail using standard MLM techniques. It's way too expensive, too competitive, and it is not duplicative.

Why MLM'ers can't keep a program going strong

MLM'ers not "sure" about MLM company or service

Often, a person will "sign up" in a MLM program in a "fit of excitement." After the dust clears, he comes down to earth and reality slowly sets in. He then starts having doubts about the company, the product or service and his own ability to promote it. If he has enrolled in a program that is not well established, he may have some well-founded fears. Therefore, it is of utmost importance for the new MLM'er to align himself with a solid company with unquestionable products and services!

> **E-Z TIP:** Follow up with your first level of people. You can do this by letter or phone. If you signed up someone who is not active, replace him with someone new, but keep all your first level people alive.

◆ *TIP:* You would be smart to pick an established, financially sound MLM company that is at least two years old with unquestionable products or services. That way, you can feel good about the company and products that you are promoting. There is nothing quite like being able to "tell the complete truth" to your prospective customers.

♦ *TRICK:* Don't select an MLM just because you are "in love" with the product. Put your emphasis on the business, the money making potential, and the capability of the company to help you promote it.

New MLM'er doesn't stick with it long enough

Starting any company takes time, and this is certainly true with MLM. By the time you study any program, write for, receive, and study the literature, and sign up, you have spent a lot of time. You then have to generate your leads, and so on. And, there is a lead time before you get your first check. It also takes time for your organization grow. And on and on. The point is, it will take several months before you can expect much of anything to start to happen. You should set in your mind that you are going to stick with this for at least one year. That just makes good business sense.

> **CAUTION** If the company is not at least two years old, things can get very shaky very quickly. Even slight financial problems or bad press can crater this company overnight.

It's also good sense to use the mail-order promotions to earn money during the interim time. That way, you are earning extra profits and generating a lot of surplus leads to help your downline. But don't spend all your initial promotional money on one thing all at once. Do a little testing. Spread it out and find out what works best for you. If you "blow it" all in one shot, and it doesn't work, then what?

When an MLM company is in serious trouble

Here is something that can happen, so you had better be prepared for it. As mentioned, there are some excellent MLM companies. But, any company can get into serious trouble, and a lot of MLM companies certainly do. They can get into financial problems, or get bad "press," have management problems, etc. Anything can happen, and if you are one of the unlucky ones to be promoting this company, you could quickly become another MLM fatality. Particularly if you are promoting only this one MLM company.

 note You can partake of several MLM companies for less than $200 a month, and still enjoy the benefits.

MLM offers many wonderful opportunities. We also know that this is a volatile industry. That doesn't mean we should not participate. But, don't invest several thousand dollars in one MLM company. Although the companies that are "highly recommended" are excellent, solid companies, they are not perfect. In fact, some may go "belly up." But not all at once! Worst case, you will be in a MLM company at least a few months or years before they get into trouble.

- ◆ *TRICK:* Sponsor your first level quickly. That way, your income will more than cover your costs. This can be done with just a little extra effort. Then show your first level how to do the same. That way, you earn profits quickly and stay ahead of the game.

- ◆ *TRAP:* Don't be an MLM "junkie" without a plan. Diversifying with a good, coherent plan is one thing, but just buying into a lot of MLM companies is a "no-no." There are many people that buy into dozens of MLM programs without promoting any of them.

How to build a secure income

When you can afford it, buy into more MLM programs and other mail-order offerings. Reinvest some of your profits and round out your MLM companies to at least three. Start promoting the original program again so you can recruit members into your new MLM programs. When you do this, you will generate surplus leads for your original MLM programs. At this point, you can either feed these leads to your existing downline, or start to build a second organization.

You may also consider forming a co-op advertising group made up of your downline. You can advertise locally or nationally. You simply put the advertising package together, and your downline pays you so much for a block advertising. They get tons of leads, and your downline pays you so much for a block of advertising—your downline builds automatically.

◆ *TRAP:* Don't forget the method that you used to succeed. After you become successful, you will want to work more closely with the individual MLM companies that you are promoting. All these companies have "grand" ways that they want

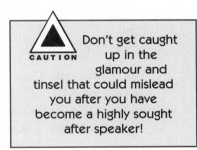

you to use and teach. Beware! Stick to the system that worked for you. If you want to become active in speaking engagements, opportunity meetings and the like, then that's another story.

More secrets to your MLM success

Multi-level marketing may be *the* opportunity of our era. Many fortunes were made, and many, many more will be made by this simple marketing method. But, it seems there are many people who gave MLM a sincere effort still were not rewarded. There are many reasons for this. Most relate to the person's personal abilities and the quality and price of the product being sold. There are ways to overcome those problems and make MLM work for you, and here is what the greats in the field have done to achieve their incredible incomes:

- **Sell only quality products at fair prices.** The company supplying the product must be reputable and offer prompt service.

- **Choose specific items or product lines that sell for under $20** and will lead to subsequent sales of the same item to the same person.

- **Show the product and give brochures to absolutely everyone** you know from your brother to your meter reader to the person at the gas company who opens your check envelope. These people will eventually come to you.

- **Always add a personal, handwritten note** with each brochure you mail. Encourage them to read the material and outline what you know about their job. Tell them what makes your opportunity so good. Get them to read the literature. Personal sales notes are incredibly powerful tools.

- **When using the mail, be careful about using mailing lists.** Most commercial lists are overpriced and pull much more poorly than advertised. It is wiser to advertise your opportunity in magazines with classified sections, especially those with other MLM ads.

- **Contact as many people as possible in a 24-hour day.** You will not get rich by getting others to make you rich. You will get rich by being successful and by demonstrating your success to others. This only comes through action.

- **Fast money in MLM is rare; big money is not so rare.** You may not even get a first check for six weeks, and it will probably be small. The aim of your efforts is to build toward a network of distributors under you, especially on the third through fifth levels, where fortunes are won and lost.

- **Plan your campaign.** Know exactly where you want to be in one month, six months, a year, five years from now. Stick with every bit of the plan you can, although you will find revisions necessary as your success grows. If your plan requires mailing X number of letters or holding X number of sales meetings a week, do it, and fill every activity with the maximum amount of efficiency and effectiveness.

> Don't waste time! The more effort you expend in the crucial first few weeks, the more rewards you will reap "downline."

- **Never let yourself stay discouraged** for more than a moment. Persistence is the real key to MLM selling. The longer and harder you work, the more certain you can be that you will win. There are still many fortunes to be made, so never blame a good product for your failure. The losers are the dabblers and the dropouts.

- **Don't stay too long with just one product or product line** without adding another—unless specifically required by your contract. Add a new line as often as your finances permit. Department stores make more money than specialty shops.

Insider secrets to your own MLM empire

7

Chapter 7

Insider secrets to your own MLM empire

What you'll find in this chapter:

➡ How to research an MLM program

➡ Cost-saving MLM strategies

➡ How coding can help

➡ A word about record-keeping

➡ 40 essential MLM rules

There are a number of appealing MLM programs available. Many look as though they could put money in your pockets. However, don't delude yourself into thinking that multi-level marketing won't cost you anything or require much time or work on your part. Indeed, successful selling for multi-level marketing requires an investment, dedication, and a lot of hard work!

However, before you "sign-up" for any deal or begin one of your own, it's going to pay you to do a little bit of market research relative to the sales potential of the whole deal. For instance, if you can sell to a "waiting market," you'll make money. But, if the people you attempt to recruit as duplicates of yourself feel that they are going to have a hard time selling it, then you haven't got much of a winning MLM program, regardless of how much money you claim they can make.

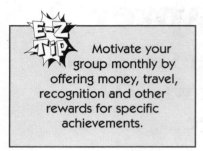

Motivate your group monthly by offering money, travel, recognition and other rewards for specific achievements.

This specifically applies to MLM programs that offer "limited appeal" products such as gourmet recipes, health foods, household "knick-knacks," books on needlecraft or magazine subscriptions. Beware also of deals that require you to purchase an inventory or maintain a certain sales level. Look for the "bad parts" of an offer, and then weigh these against the ease with which you'll be able to make a sale. At the bottom line, if you have a hard time selling it, then the people you recruit to sell it for you will find it even harder to sell, and that will be the end of your "big money" multi-level program.

There are countless reports, manuals, books and other publications that "supposedly" tell you how to attain riches in mail order, party plan selling, and even street-corner sales. The thing is, all of these "how-to" publications try to instruct you on how to put a mailing piece together, how often to send your offers out, and even the importance of "neatness & quality" within your offer, but very few if any come right out and help you get your offer to your most likely customers. As you know, unless an interested buyer sees your offer, you're not going to make any money.

note Be persistent— only one out of every 20 people you approach may get serious about the business or be interested in your products.

What I'm saying is that most people thrash around, waste time, spend hundreds of dollars, and never make any money simply because they don't know how to get their offers to the people—without it costing them an arm and a leg.

Here's how it's done: Regardless of what your offer entails, put together the most dynamic and mass-appeal "one-page" advertising circular you can come up with. The best-selling and most-productive circular is one that "tells the reader you have a solution to his money problems." In other words, with your circular, promise him a way to make himself rich, and he'll not only be interested, he'll jump on your program.

Next make it as easy as possible for the people who see your offer to respond. That is, in addition to an order coupon at the bottom of the advertising circular describing your offer, give him the chance to get involved in your program for the least possible cost.

> *note* Keep in touch— communicate by newsletter, meetings, weekly calls, postcards, voice mail—pass on pertinent information immediately.

If you put together a "winning offer," most people seeing it will want to know more about it, but if you charge them $5 for registration or enrollment fees, you'll lose about half of those "wanting in," because they're afraid of being ripped off. But if you charge them $2 or less, almost all of the people seeing your offer will "take a chance," just to find out what kind of a deal it is you're offering.

note In summary, you must have a one-page advertising circular that really appeals to most of the people—*your chance to solve all your money problems!* It must include a coupon the reader clips off and sends in to you for enrollment or registration in your program. It has to be priced at $2 or less to "get everybody" to at least check it out. And, it must be complete on one page to hold your printing costs in line.

EZ TIP Concentrate on what you can do for your distributors and customers, not on your own profits.

Assuming you're with us, and organized thus far, take this advertising circular you created to a quick printer in your area. Ask the shop to print up 10,000 of these one page advertising circulars for you. This will cost you approximately $200.

If you don't have the money, you can either work an arrangement with the printer to pay him in 30 days, or include him in as a "silent partner" in your program. Ask him to read over your offer, explain how you intend to get it to the people, and about how much money you expect to gross from it. Then, simply offer to split the proceeds if he'll carry your printing costs for you.

While the circulars are being printed, and the ink is drying, line up your initial distribution efforts. The first thing is to contact youth groups and organizations in your area. Arrange with the leaders of these groups to pay them $10 per thousand if they'll station people at the exits to all the shopping centers in your area and pass out one of your circulars to everyone as they leave the shopping center. Simply tell them that you've got 10,000 of these circulars to hand out, and that you'll pay them $100 for handing them out on the first of the month.

> **E-Z TIP**
> Send customers monthly promotional information. Don't forget your customers and don't let your customers forget you!

The best kind of places to distribute your circulars are those near discount stores, recycled clothing stores, and inventory reduction sales. Next on your list of places to hand out circulars should be flea markets, swap and shop events, and even garage sales. Anywhere there are a lot of people congregating is a good place to hand out your advertising circulars—all in your own hometown and without postage costs.

> **note**
> Believe in your products so much that you know every person you talk to is going to buy from you.

Now comes the good part—while your "hired helpers" are handing circulars out for you at strategic locations throughout the area, you should be calling in person on every shopkeeper and store owner or manager in the area.

Show them each a copy of your circular. Explain your program, and offer to cut them in on the profits if they'll help you by dropping one in with the purchases of each of their customers. The stores won't want to become involved in extra bookkeeping nor the handling of money for you, so you'll

Approach former top producers. They are always open.

have to devise a method of knowing where your orders come from—a code for each of the stores handing out circulars for you.

This is very simple. Just assign a different "department number" to each store. When you have the circulars printed, insert that department code in the return address.

Generally speaking, you should offer to supply the circulars free to the distributors, including the "special coding" for each store. Thus, the need for a good working relationship with a printer in your area. The amount of commission per order received that you allow to each store should range between 15 and 30 percent, but of course, always try to finalize each deal for the least amount.

Be sure to keep good records of all your incoming orders. It would be wise to have a separate record book for each distributor. Thus, you can review the number of orders received from each distributor's customers with him when you pay his commission at the end of each month. At the same time, you should jot on a 3 X 5 index card

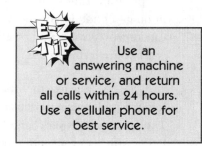

Use an answering machine or service, and return all calls within 24 hours. Use a cellular phone for best service.

the name, address and phone number of each person sending in an order. Arrange these cards in alphabetical and zip code order, and store them in an old shoebox. When you have 10, 15, or 25,000 of them, you'll be able to sell them at $1 per name to any number of mailing list brokers.

From each envelope you receive, clip the stamp off and save these in still another shoebox. Stamp collectors will pay you $10 to $25 for each shoebox full of stamps you collect. After you've clipped the stamps off, place these envelopes with your customer's return address in still another storage box. Then you have several boxes full of these envelopes from people who spent money with you. There are any number of "list buyers" who will pay you for them.

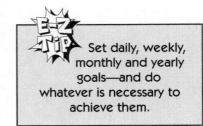

Set daily, weekly, monthly and yearly goals—and do whatever is necessary to achieve them.

Once you have your town saturated with circular distributors—be sure to leave a stack in all the barber shops and beauty salons, as well as at the counter in cafe restaurants, bowling centers, theaters, and the "lodges" of all the fraternal as well as labor unions—your next move is simply to duplicate these efforts in a neighboring town or city.

DEFINITION

Basically, we're talking about multi-level marketing and total advertising-recruiting efforts on your part. Your main thrust should be to "pull in" as many people as possible—show them the program, and if they want it, let them get in on it—if not, forget about them and move on to the next prospect. This is called *prospecting,* and it's going to cost you money and time, regardless of what you're trying to sell.

So, you put together an "invitation type announcement" which is your initial $2 advertising circular, and you get it to as many people as possible. They pay you a "cover charge" of $2 to find out what your program is all about. Before you get upset and throw this book in the wastebasket, think about this: Let's suppose there are 42,000 people in your town—30,000 adults, and 18,000 separate families. If each of these 18,000 families were to send you $2, how much money would you have? $36,000 right?

The people send you $2 for a "look-see" at your program to solve their money problems. You send them back your multi-level program brochure which describes how they can duplicate what you're doing and make a bundle of money for themselves, and tells them the cost of supplies to get started. At the same time, you send out another one-page advertising circular that offers business success reports. Just as another for instance, let's say that 30% of the people receiving your MLM brochure enroll and send for a start-up kit or supplies. You've expanded your MLM distributorship and made money, right? Now, let's suppose that of all the people who sent $2 to find out what your program is all about, a total of 40% spend $5 with you for one of your business success reports—$36,000 gross income for initial expenses of $600—then, let's say your MLM brochures cost you $100 per thousand, for total expenses

Give yourself a reward for reaching your goal and a penalty for falling short.

thus far of $2,400—plus another $600 for your business success reports circulars—with another $11,250 as your commission from these reports, for a total gross income thus far of $47,250. Then, third class postage and envelopes cost $2,550. Subtract your expenses from your gross income of $47,250 and you should end up taking $41,700 to your bank, catching up on your bills, or spending on a long overdue vacation to Acapulco or Hawaii.

That's it! That's how easy and simple it is and it actually works! Once you cover your entire state in this manner, simply start renting mailing lists of people listed as Opportunity Seekers, and shotgun your basic one-page, $2 offer to all of them.

I used a standard "$2 circular" for some time now, and it's proven to be a fantastic winner for me from the start. I had 10,000 printed at a cost of $200— paid a couple of Cub Scout troops $100 to hand them out for me; and from that initial 10,000 circulars, I received 2,341 $2 inquiries = $4,682 . . . and, another 33 orders for the MLM Manual offered on the same circular = $7,060— total income from our initial $300 investment was $11,742. Since that time, I expanded my market, and I'm now putting out 10,000 of these circulars each and every week.

You can do it too! All it takes is that first circular and then, total distribution.

Here are the 40 essential rules you must learn to make even more money in MLM. Follow these rules every day.

1) Use your products regularly.

2) Make a total commitment to your program for at least one year.

3) Sell yourself first, then the products and the marketing plan.

4) Spend 90% of your business time with distributors, customers and prospects.

5) Present your products and marketing plan personally to at least one person daily.

6) Let everyone know what business you are in. Advertise.

7) Make "understanding people" more important that product knowledge.

8) Duplicate yourself by making distributors independent of you.

9) Praise your distributor's accomplishments.

10) Mingle with top distributors and ask how they made it.

11) Lead by example. Never stop recruiting, training and retailing.

12) Keep it simple: do things others can easily duplicate and copy.

13) Conduct simple, brief, dramatic presentations.

14) Listen 80% of the time, talk 20%.

15) Satisfy all complaints immediately.

16) Ask for referrals from your best customers.

17) Give customers more than they expect. Everyone loves a free gift.

18) Develop at least 30 retail and/or wholesale customers.

19) Provide one-day delivery service.

20) Tell your customers how much you appreciate their business.

21) Don't accept "no" as a final answer—approach each prospect at least 12 times a year with new information.

22) Speak enthusiastically about your business and products.

23) Work on top priority projects that produce the highest returns.

24) Build your list of contacts daily while you build your reputation.

25) Fit the needs of a prospect with the benefits of your products and/or business opportunity.

26) Organize your files so you can locate any piece of information in 30 seconds.

27) Do not pass negative rumors downline! Check the facts yourself.

28) Listen to cassette tapes on multi-level tips from top earners.

29) Subscribe to multi-level magazines. Read self-help books.

30) Expand your distributorship world-wide. Think big!

31) Tell others what they are interested in knowing, not what you think they should hear.

32) Spend money on things that will make you more money.

33) Schedule important tasks at your best time of day.

34) Delegate—do those things only you can do.

35) Read biographies of successful people to be inspired by their lives.

36) Present business opportunities and training regularly.

37) Plow your profits back into building your business.

38) Know that if others can do it, so can you. Challenge yourself.

39) Have so much fun in your business that others want to join you.

40) Do it now!

Build a money-making MLM machine on a shoestring

8

Chapter 8

Build a money-making MLM machine on a shoestring

What you'll find in this chapter:

➠ Mail-order techniques

➠ How to combine MLM with mail-order

➠ What successful mail-order dealers do

➠ Why you need to make up-front money

➠ A simple plan for working mail-order

How to go broke promoting MLM by mail

note

Let's review how MLM companies operate in general. Mostly, all quality MLM companies have first class promotional material and services that you can use, including expensive full color literature, audio tapes, video tapes, local and national meetings, training seminars and the like. They encourage you to have #800 phone numbers, voice box mail services and FAX machines. This is all geared primarily to sponsor local people. And it works when you are primarily selling face to face. But, none of this is worth a "plugged nickel" if you are trying to sell by mail. It's way too expensive.

Here's how the typical MLM "big time" promoter can lose a lot of money. First, he signs up in a wonderful MLM program. Next, he decides to sponsor as many people as he can. (Surely, if he gets 100 people in his first level, he can get thousands in his organization? Wrong!) To sponsor 100 people fast, he advertises in *USA Today* under "Business Opportunities." Ninety percent of all ads in this section are MLM companies and distributors. He gets to spend about $500 for a tiny ad. Next, he gets a voice box mail service with a pre-recorded message. Now, he sits back and, sure enough, he gets about 50 to 100 leads. (That's $5 to $10 a lead cost!). Guess what next? He has about 100 leads that he must call back at HIS cost! He'll probably have to call several times to catch these people. Another cost of $5 to $10 for everyone that he talks to. Sure enough, some of the people are genuinely interested and they want more information and literature.

Remember that expensive literature I told you about? Now, he has to send it. He has to send the expensive $10 to $20 video with the expensive literature. Otherwise, he can't possibly "sign" anyone up without meeting him face to face. So be it. Send it all out. Now we're up to $30 to $50 cost on just this one person! Whew! Oh well, we have now sent out the expensive packages and we'll see what happens? Probably nothing. That's what follow-up phone calls are for. Another cost. More time. If he is lucky, he will finally sign up one or two new distributors.

What a messy, costly way to do this!

If you want to succeed in MLM using standard MLM techniques you need to:

- Handle multiple MLM programs

- Recruit well for your first level

- Have a duplicative method

- Build a deep organization

- Help and train your first level

- Sell locally first, then expand

Mail-order techniques

Let's now see how differently the professional mail-order dealers operate.

First, the basic idea in mail-order is to get as many customers as possible so you can sell to your customers repeatedly. The very first objective in mail-order is to develop your own customer base. Once you have a customer base, you can keep sending them your new offers or catalogs and keep reselling them.

No professional mail-order dealer will ever attempt to make a "killing" with advertising or mass mail to non-customers. It just doesn't happen. They will, however, do a lot of advertising and mass mailings to build their customer base, which is pure gold! These customers like to deal with you and they buy again . . . and again . . .

Definition:
Professional mail-order dealers talk in terms of the *front end* and *back end*. The front end is the method of simply getting customers—even at no profit or at a slight loss.

and again. As long as you have several offers. That brings up another fundamental point. To succeed in mail-order, as with any business, you must have several products or offers to sell. If you don't, you will most likely lose money in trying.

When it comes to advertising, these guys are pros. All use tiny classified ads like what you see in the back of national advertising. If these ads get results, they test and test and then place small one inch ads. When they have an offer and a publication fit, they might place a large ad. Only then. You will rarely see them advertise in *USA Today*. Way too expensive!

DEFINITION

They will use *leader items*. A leader item is an inexpensive report or item that typically sells for less than $5.00. By advertising a leader item that costs $2.00 or $3.00, you can expect to get orders directly. The objective is to break even with your mailing and advertising costs and build your customer base.

Reprintable reports are excellent for this. Sometimes you can actually make money right up front if you have a "HOT" item. Everyone that buys the leader item will then get more literature included. It generally goes postage FREE! Do you see how they operate? Slowly, but surely. Making money as they go. Testing and re-testing.

Let me recap what successful mail-order dealers will do.

+ develop as many customers as they can

+ promote nationally

+ have several offerings

+ have cost effective ways to generate customers

> **note** Some reports say that there are over 50,000 small mail-order dealers quietly earning over $50,000 a year operating out of their homes.

How to combine MLM with mail-order

If you look at the "recaps" above, you will not find many common ties between MLM and mail-order—do you? Yet, there are a lot of amateurish MLM distributors and companies that try to promote MLM by mail without understanding the first basic principle of mail-order techniques. It can be done. With astounding results.

Do you see some of the main differences between promoting MLM and mail-order? In MLM you "sign up" only a few people, no more than 10, on your first level. With mail-order, you want to develop as many customers as you can. With MLM, you want to sell locally, and with mail-order, you have to sell nationally. With MLM, you are told to be loyal to just one company, but with mail-order, you should have many offerings.

Wouldn't it be nice to be able to take all the good techniques from both MLM and from mail-order techniques and throw away the nasty ones? Well, that's just what these chapters are all about. Mail-order dealers operate lean and mean. If they don't make a profit on everything that they do, they are out of business. That's a good premise to start with.

> Don't do anything unless you can make some up-front money, or at least break even. If mail-order dealers were to make deals like a lot of MLM distributors do, they would be out of business immediately.

Below are a few examples. Avoid them like the plague! Remember—the offer that is made must be duplicated (by you), if it is any good.

- "Join my program and I'll pay your way in." What a miserable offer! This guy is willing to pay his money to get me into his program. What is he really saying? If I join him, I have to pay for my new people? This can't get any worse.

- "Sure, I'll send you the information FREE." Now let's see. If he sends me videos and expensive literature, I bet that is costing him at least $10 to $20. Hmmm. If I get into this program, does this mean that I have to send out this FREE stuff? At my cost? No way.

- "Join now, and I will build your downline." This guy is absolutely naive or just a flat-out liar. It is impossible for him to build your downline. And you cannot possibly duplicate this method. Watch your wallet and stay away.

While you may be able to help a few select people by "signing up" a few people for them, you cannot possibly do this for your entire downline! You must provide a logical method so that your people can do this for themselves!

How to sell MLM by mail

Now that you understand the fundamentals of MLM and mail-order techniques, let's see what it takes to promote MLM by mail. In all cases, you need to come up with a plan that makes sense, one that is good for you and can grow. If you are going to promote MLM programs by mail, wouldn't it make sense to operate your core business like a mail-order business? For now, here is a simplified step-by-step way to do this:

+ Start a mail-order business selling reprintable reports by mail.

2. Make money generating leads with postcards and mini-flyers.

+ Make several offers. You will have developed a customer base and MANY leads. Now you can start making BIG money with repeat offerings.

+ Promote several MLM companies at the same time. That way, you can sign up one person in several programs. You will be amazed how you can make money with this method.

+ Build your MLM programs deep! For the MLM programs that you are promoting, try to get no more than 10 or so people active on your first level. Then show them how to use this plan.

+ Sell your literature! By using mail-order techniques, you will have generated a lot of leads. The people requesting literature will pay you to send this literature to them.

+ Sell your MLM leads to your downline. That way, you get your downline off and running quickly. After you have 10 or so people in your first level, you will have probably generated hundreds of extra leads. Usually, you want to sell these leads to your downline. Remember, your system must be duplicative. And profitable.

+ Sell the reports to your downline. That way, they become automatically trained, and you make a buck selling the reports to them.

✦ Choose MLM programs that have literature that is cost effective to send out by mail.

✦ Do not compete with your 10 people in your first level. Once you have active people, share your success methods with them. That is, show them how to use these reports. If you have advertised, let them know what did best for you. If you do this right, you may want to back out of the mail-order business, and just let your 10 MLM downline people carry on.

The MLM money tree

Chapter 9

The MLM money tree

Multi-level marketing is definitely the way to go for people aspiring to have more money. Most of the world's leading economic forecasters say that fully 75% of the world's consumer business will eventually be conducted via multi-level marketing plans.

The thing to do is to learn all you can about this method of selling—how it works and why it works—and then to get going with a multi-level marketing program that can accumulate a fortune for you. Make no mistake about it, multi-level marketing has made a lot of people very rich already, and will make a lot more people even richer in the coming years.

Multi-level marketing is based upon the idea of each person involved selling to his or her friends, with each of these people in turn introducing their friends into the program. It's definitely an "endless chain" idea that has unlimited money-making potential.

Theoretically, everybody knows or comes into contact with an average of 100 different people each week. If only 10 of those people were to give you $10 per week, you would have an income of $100 per week. And then, if these people were to duplicate your efforts, passing back to you $1 for each new person they enlisted in the program, your income would soon become astronomical!

Undoubtedly, you heard the story of how you can become rich simply by saving a penny a day, and doubling it each day for 30 days. Then, there are the pyramid or chain letter schemes that we've all been offered. Multi-level marketing, in principle, works the same way, with the only difference being in the product offered for sale.

> *note*
> MLM works because everybody wants to become rich. It's an idea that anyone—regardless of education, background or basic financial status—can perpetuate from the privacy of his or her own home.

Most multi-level programs make a big splash when they are first introduced, and then quickly die out. However, the concept of initiating a program that sells itself via an endless chain will always be popular because it holds the promise of bringing riches if the chain isn't broken.

note Multi-level marketing is appealing because an opportunity for all the participants to get rich with a minimum investment and very little time, effort, or involvement.

The basic fallacy of multi-level marketing is overestimating the number of people each individual participant can easily enlist into the program. After you talk to all your relatives, your neighbors, co-workers, and friends across town, you're more or less stymied for new people to bring into the program.

The bottom line is simply that you cannot recruit everybody you talk to—in fact, if you enlist 10% of the people you attempt to interest in the program, you'll be doing well. You're going to get some rejections, and these rejections are basically what turns most people off—deflates their ego, drains their enthusiasm, and in the end, is the primary reason they drop out.

Regardless of what you sell, you must always have a goal in mind—you intend to sell 10 units of a product or recruit 10 new people into your program between now and the first of the month. You have to believe that you can do it—want to do it—and then get out and beat the bushes until you do it! Once you've achieved this first goal, you should take a day off and reward yourself with a night on the town or by splurging on something you've always wanted.

Then, after setting a goal for yourself, and proving that you can achieve it, you should set a new goal for yourself—if you recruited 10 new people into your program last month, then this month, you're going to bring in 15 new members.

You're going to make the really big money in multi-level marketing by selling "business start-up kits," and not really from spending time inspiring or motivating the people you've already brought into the program. In other words, sell the program to as many people as possible, and count on the motivational and money-making opportunities within your dealer start-up kit to cause them to put forth the effort to get out and try to make some

> **note** To be successful in selling—and this is the secret to multi-level riches—you must present your program to as many people as possible. Close the sale with your first presentation, and let the buyer either get with it, or die from his own lack of initiative.

money on their own. In the end, and as the old saying goes: you can lead a horse to water, but you can't make him drink it—any time and/or energy you spend "calling back" the people you've already sold is going to cost you money and limit your gross income.

It's as simple as that—the more people to whom you present your program, the more sales you're going to make.

Obviously, if you spend all your time on the telephone inviting people over to a Special Opportunity Party at your house, and then another 3 hours presenting your program to them, it's going to take you a long time to present your program to 10,000 people and make $10,000. And, your costs to rent a hall—advertise—and present a seminar program—will amount to more than you take in.

> *note*
>
> You should have some idea of how mail order works—what makes it profitable and the reasons why—and with this understanding, combine the "easy riches" appeal of your multi-level program with mail order selling.

If you have the initial promotional abilities, the credit and/or cash, and a really dynamic program— you can make it big, and quickly, by staging seminar-type meetings at the rate of 3 to 5 per week. Still, this is expensive and time consuming—a lot of work on your part, and not the easiest, most profitable way to go.

The only logical way to go—to reach as many people as possible for the least amount of money and effort on your part—is via the mails. In other words, the marrying of your multi-level marketing efforts to mail order will be the least expensive and most profitable for you.

You can send out 50,000 sales letters and multi-level program brochures in one month, and theoretically make $50,000 from an expenditure of $10,000 or less—a return of $5 for every dollar invested, which isn't bad.

Here's our recommendation:

✦ **Write a short, one-page report outlining the basic Success Secrets of Multi-level Marketing.** You can tag-line this report with an invitation for the readers to send for a complete or more detailed manual or tape relative to multi-level marketing how to; a directory or current listing of money-making multi-level programs; or even a listing of other reports relative to money-making home-based businesses you have for sale.

✦ **Advertise.** Once you have such a report, the next thing for you to do is advertise. Write an ad such as: FREE REPORT!... Money-making secrets of multi-level marketers. SASE to _____ (your name, address, city, state, zip).

✦ **Place this ad in one of the national publications** carrying lots of mail order advertisements—such as The National Enquirer, American Business, Money-making Opportunities, Entrepreneur, Income Opportunities, Specialty Salesman or any one of the hundreds of other such publications.

✦ **Make response cards.** In reply to each SASE you receive, first list the name and address of each respondent, along with the date received and what you send back to them, on 3 by 5 cards. Arrange these cards in zip code and alphabetical order, and store them in an old shoe box. Then, with your one-page report and a multi-level marketing brochure—stuff the envelopes and drop them in your nearest mailbox.

If your ad runs in The National Enquirer, you could expect to get 1,000 or more responses each time it runs. So far, your cost is for the ad—the printing of the one page report—and your multi-level program brochures. From these 1,000 free reports you send out you should be able to convert about 300 into new members into the multi-level program you're promoting.

E-Z TIP: Contract to run such an ad over three issues. This gives your ad maximum exposure, and should result in an overwhelming number of responses for you.

Thus, for an initial cost of $30 for the ad—$100 for the MLM brochures—and the time it takes you to stuff the envelopes—300 buyers at $10 each will give you a gross of $3,000. That's how you parlay your multi-level program into a fortune, using mail-order selling techniques.

One very important thing to always remember, relative to starting a new business: You cannot take any money coming in from your business advertising and use it to pay your "everyday" bills. In other words, you cannot expect to use this money to live on—you have to pour it back into your business to perpetuate that flow of income.

Whenever you advertise, in addition to replies to your offer, you can expect a "ton of mail" from other people trying to interest you in what they're selling. Basically, you should go through all of the "junk mail" and look it over, save the stuff that looks interesting, is well done, or that you can learn from, and perhaps "lift" some ideas from them for use in your own selling efforts.

Compile the names of the people and/or companies sending you these offers. Just as with those replying to your advertised offer, jot down the date and a short description of the material received—then send them a sales letter/brochure about your multi-level program. In sending sales letters/brochures to these people, you don't have to send them immediately. You can list these people in an "incoming offer notebook," and then include them with your regular direct mail packages you send. But for sure, clip the stamps and save the incoming envelopes along with those from your bona fide replies.

> *note* The important thing is to present your offer to as many different people as possible—particularly to those people with an itch to get rich quick.

◆ Increase your advertising.

So you spent $150 and made about $3,000 in a period of about three months. Now you want to perpetuate this income, and build it to twice that amount coming in every month. What you do is take the income from that first ad, and increase your advertising. In other words, use it to buy ad space in as many other publications as possible.

If your first $150 brought in $3,000 from exposure in just one publication, presumably $2,000 will bring you $50,000 from exposure in 10 different publications. Continue multiplying your advertising exposure and it won't be long before you will be "snowed under" with dollar bills, checks and money orders. Remember this, though: You cannot spend any of that money on yourself until the business is bringing in several thousand dollars per month on a regular basis. You have to pour it back into the business in order to allow your business to reach its full potential.

✦ **Make a one-page "Money Tree" circular**, similar to that included as reference material at the end of this chapter. Be sure that you keep the cost $2 or less to "find out about the program." Then, with a listing of money-making reports such as ours—printed on the back of your "Money Tree" circular— shotgun this out to as many people as possible.

You may have outstanding success handing them out at local shopping centers, passing them out door-to-door, and by including them as "ride alongs" with a bulk mailing program.

 In addition to circulating your "Money Tree" flyers by hand, you should rent or buy—on a regular basis—as many different mailing lists of income opportunity seekers as you can afford, and shotgun one of your circulars to each of these names. You can also find inexpensive mailing list suppliers in just about any publication that carries mail order advertising.

For sure, you should spend the money to obtain a 3rd class bulk rate mailing permit, and then use it to send out all your mailings. Start by sending out 250 pieces per week, and then gradually increase your volume to the point where you're sending out 5,000 or more pieces per week, and you'll be in business.

✦ **Follow up your offers.** Send a copy of your free report, plus your multi-level marketing brochure to people who follow up on your offer. You can stop there if you want, but there's lots more money to be made just from these initial efforts.

note The secret to getting rich in mail order has to do with presenting a free offer most people find hard to pass up. You make your money from whatever you send in reply to those taking you up on the free offer.

Follow-up on offers to people who themselves are out beating the bushes to drum up extra income. When you receive all these names and addresses of people interested in receiving a report on multi-level marketing, compile the names and rent or sell them to other multi-level operators. Do this simply by making a one-page sales letter type of flyer or circular, offering your names for rent at whatever price you want to charge, and then by including this flyer in your outgoing mail.

Besides including your "Money Tree" circular, and the mailing list rental offer, you should also include a one page circular describing and offering for sale a list of your money-making reports. Then, by soliciting co-op mailings from other mail order operators, you'll have a "pretty full" envelope of offers going out.

note Finally, the one thing you must always bear in mind is how your mailing package looks to the person receiving it. Your envelopes should be professionally printed with your return address—your sales letters should be written to impress the recipient; no misspelled words or smudges from erasures or worn out typewriters; and your included coupons or offers must have eye appeal. By all means, the quality of your multi-level brochure is important. Although multiple colored printing does tend to pull better than

CAUTION Photo-copying your offers and hoping for the best just won't do. The more affluent you appear to be, from your envelope to each offer contained within, the better your chances of making a sale.

just black and white, you can do very well starting with black and white materials so long as the image you project is professional.

That's how it's done—you can take these methods, maybe even improve upon them a bit, and make tons of money—or you can set everything aside and tell yourself that you'll get started on it next week. The instructions are valid and the opportunity is here and now—whatever you do is up to you.

Sample Money Tree circular

How would you like to own your own money tree?

A never-ending supply of money for the next 10-20-30-even 50 years!

Money to meet all your monthly obligations . . . Money to invest . . . Money to enjoy the finer things in life . . . It can all be yours now.

This is what we're offering: Our all new Multi-Level Marketing Program is being acclaimed as the most dynamic money-making opportunity available!

Unlike other multi-level programs you may have heard of, with our marketing concept, there's no prospecting to worry about . . . no selling required—no parties to organize—no sales meetings to attend . . . no bookkeeping to bog you down.

Basically, all you have to do is join up and let the money start rolling in. Really, all that's necessary is a $2 Sponsorship Fee, and your agreement to pass along one of these circulars to other people you think would be interested in obtaining financial security.

The program is simple and easy—requires no training or experience—and only $2 to start you on the road to the really big money!

Let me repeat—All we want you to do is duplicate and pass along this circular to other people you think are interested in obtaining financial security!

Just tear off the coupon below, and send it in today. By immediate return mail, we send you all the details on this exciting new money-making opportunity, plus a couple of SUPER BONUSES, and a Master Copy of this circular so you can start making money for yourself right away—without further delay!

There's a lot of people using the multi-level concept to haul in $1,000 . . . $5,000 . . . even $10,000 per month! With this program, you can do it too!

We studied the methods of Amway, Enhance, Shaklee and most of the others—none come close to the huge profits our program offers! Until now, the "inside secrets" of how the really big money is made in multi-level marketing were TOP SECRET, but no more—In addition to the opportunity to start making more money than you've ever seen before in your life—for a small Sponsorship Fee of just $2—we're offering our manual *How to Build Your Own Million Dollar Multi-level Empire* for just $20.

Never before has so much about the inside secrets of multi-level marketing been revealed in such a simple and straight-forward manner. And we guarantee that with the information in this manual, you can do it too! This step-by-step manual frankly reveals how you can immediately start making all the money you want—in your spare time, without leaving the comforts or privacy of your own home! All, via multi-level marketing!

Complete the coupon below, and get it in to us now!!!

OKAY! I'm ready for some extra money. Here's my two dollars—sign me up, and send me the full details on your money-making multi-level deal!

_____I'm also including an additional $20 for your manual on how I can build my own *Million Dollar Multi-Level Empire*... Please Rush!!!

$2 enclosed by cash_____ check_____ money-order_____ for sign-up only.

$22 enclosed by cash_____ check_____ money-order_____ for sign-up and multi-level manual.

MEMBER NAME:_____

STREET:_____

CITY:_____ STATE:_____ ZIP:_____

How to make a fortune with post-cards

10

Chapter 10

How to make a fortune with post-cards

If you have an offer to make to the public, a postcard is very often the simplest, fastest and most inexpensive way to get your message out. Anyone can circulate postcards. That means that kids and teenagers can help out in many ways. Another advantage of using a postcard is that you can use the copy of a postcard to print small flyers. In that way, you can print these "mini-flyers" for a fraction of a penny, while postcards cost you about 1 to 3.5 cents each, depending upon the quality that you have printed.

> **note**
> Shopping and business areas are perfect places to circulate postcards.

If you are promoting an MLM company, the power of generating quality leads by circulating postcards locally is extremely effective, if you have a good offer. You also earn a profit while you are generating these leads!

How to make money immediately with postcards

Probably the most important aspect of using a postcard is that you can easily sell a $2.00 report directly. In other words, if you offer an inexpensive item, like a report, you can generate orders simply by circulating postcards or mini-flyers. Therefore, you can circulate postcards immediately, receive orders directly, and then fill your orders yourself. You keep the money up front. Most often, you then sell additional items to your customers that buy your $2.00 report. That's how you can earn substantial additional profits. By using this method, you earn a small profit while you generate larger profits from repeat business. If you promote MLM program(s), you can then earn a serious income.

> **E-Z TIP**
>
> The easiest and fastest way to make money with postcards and "mini-flyers" is to circulate them in your local neighborhood.

Compare that method to companies that mail out postcards that offer free material. They spend a lot of money up front on postage, and a lot more in sending out the free material. You can spend a lot of money and time by doing that. By using our plan, you can actually make money up front while generating leads for other offers that you may be making.

Why it is best to circulate post cards locally

If you happen to offer a product or service that is also available from other companies, it is sometimes difficult to promote this nationally because you might be competing with many other people. This happens all the time in the mail-order business and for distributors promoting MLM programs. If these people advertise, they may very likely be competing with several other companies that are advertising in the same publication . . . with the very same advertisement. The same risk is true if mass mailings are attempted. In this case, several companies wind up sending identical literature to the same person.

I bet you have received several offers that were identical from different companies. Therefore, when you are first starting out, you have a better chance to succeed if you do it locally. That way, your offer is seen by eager people who have not seen a similar offer.

Also, if you are promoting an MLM program, you only need to sponsor a few active people, and then show these people how to do likewise.

The very best and most effective way to get started is to simply pass out a few postcards and mini-flyers in your local area. For example, let's consider MLM programs that you may want to promote. If your objective is to sponsor 10 people into this program as quickly as you can, and do it without much time or money, start locally first. The powerful concept behind this postcard promotion is that each of you personally sponsors just a few people . . . not millions! Therefore, circulate a few hundred postcards or mini-flyers in your local neighborhood, and then let your downline continue on.

Since this offer was probably not seen in your neighborhood, it is a new, fresh opportunity for anyone looking at it. That way, of your postcards are both highly effective and cost effective. Look at these advantages to starting locally:

- you can start now
- you get fast results
- it's inexpensive
- it's easy
- you can distribute as many as you want

- your downline can do it

- there's little local competition

- there is no national competition

- you can have kids do the work

Where & how to circulate postcards locally

 Pay kids to help. If you pay kids a penny or two for each postcard they circulate, you can circulate 1,000 for only $10 or $20. Compare that to at least $200 for mailing them. If you get two kids, and drive them through your neighborhood, they can cover a lot of streets in a few hours. Kids can circulate postcards by hand—either handing them to people personally or placing them on doors and/or cars:

- ✦ through newspaper delivery drivers

- ✦ door to door

- ✦ newspaper boxes—Note: It is illegal to place in mail boxes.

- ✦ under hotel room doors

- ✦ personally distribute at high consumer traffic areas

- ✦ shopping area parking lots

- ✦ hotels & motels

- ✦ sports arenas

- ✦ public parking lots

- ✦ airport parking lots

- ✦ convention centers

- ✦ hospitals

+ bowling alleys

+ night clubs

+ fine restaurants

+ schools

+ colleges

+ theaters

+ tourist attractions

+ fairs

+ large flea markets

+ auction locations

+ fast food restaurants

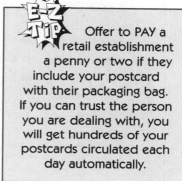

Offer to PAY a retail establishment a penny or two if they include your postcard with their packaging bag. If you can trust the person you are dealing with, you will get hundreds of your postcards circulated each day automatically.

How & where to distribute postcards yourself

The following are places to consider placing a small stack of 10 to 20 postcards. In many of these places you can simply place them with no permission. Others, you want to get permission, and in doing so you will have the opportunity to review the postcard offer with the person in charge. For example, let's say you want to place a stack of cards on the counter of your favorite convenience store. You simply say to the person in charge, "Do you mind if I leave a few of these cards here?"

If the retailer wants to know what they are, you have a good chance of explaining the program and perhaps selling the program to him.

If you look around, you will find all kinds of places where you can place a stack of 10 or so of your postcards. When you circulate your postcards this way, it is a good idea to code the location with a number so you can tell which places are working for you. You can then check on these locations every week or so and keep them replenished.

Literature racks

Literature racks are perfect for distributing your literature. Do you have any of those public literature rack areas in your large supermarkets? If so, this is one of the first places to put your literature. This is a good example of why you want to code your literature, so you can tell which locations are working best for you.

- supermarkets

- anywhere there is a magazine rack

- hotels

- libraries

- airports

- inside shopping malls

- large buildings

- hospitals

- reception and waiting lobbies

> ⚠️ **CAUTION** Make sure that you adhere to your local laws and regulations when you are circulating literature. If you have questions, check with your local authorities.

Any spots where people are waiting in lobbies are excellent! These people are trying to pass time and will read anything they can get their hands on. Ideal lobbies include:

+ automobile service center

+ tire stores

+ beauty salons

+ barber shops

+ doctor offices

- dentist offices
- medical centers
- company lobbies
- restaurant waiting areas
- hotel & motel lobbies
- airport waiting areas
- bus terminals

Retail counters of:

- convenience stores
- gas stations
- gift shops
- book stores
- video stores
- restaurant counters
- any small privately owned retail outlet

Bulletin Boards:

- libraries
- public auction notice boards
- government buildings
- post office
- factory bulletin boards
- office bulletin boards

+ travel rest areas

+ high schools

+ colleges

+ restroom bulletin boards

+ truck stops

+ make your own place and attach them to telephone poles, elevators, etc.

+ unemployment offices

More places . . .

> **E-Z TIP**
> Hand your postcards to people exhibiting at flea markets and mingle with the crowd. The people with booths are perfect candidates since they are trying to earn extra money, part time, on the side.

• computer bulletin boards

• trade shows. Here you pass out cards to the exhibitors or get there early and leave a few at each booth table. Mingle with the crowd and personally pass out cards. And don't forget the bulletin boards, the windshields, and hotels, etc.

• county fairs. There are tons of people to mingle with.

• business opportunity meetings. If you watch your newspaper, or visit a few hotels, you may find several locations where business groups regularly attend. This is fairly standard practice with the multilevel marketing groups where new people are constantly invited to an "opportunity meeting."

Consider these places so you can mingle and distribute postcards personally or to place on:

• windshields

• Here's a powerful one that I won't even count! Telephone Booths. Place your literature on any flat shelf. Do you think you can find 100 or so telephone booths? Go for it!

There you have it . . . terrific ways to circulate postcards postage free. When you mail a postcard, it goes by first class mail for less cost than a first class stamp. It is sent fast, and if there is a problem with the address, it is returned to you FREE of charge.

Your warm inner circle

Everyone has lots of friends, relatives and business associates. This is sometimes referred to as *your warm inner circle.* The standard MLM approach is for you to try to sell to your sphere of influence or your inner circle. The nice thing about this postcard program is that you don't have to personally try to sell anyone anything. Instead, you just write a short note on the front of the postcard (there's space for this) and send it off to the people that you know. consider writing a note like this, "John, I thought you might like a copy of this—Mary." Don't make the mistake of giving this plan away.

If you do, it will defeat your whole program. Make a list of everyone that you can think of that might appreciate knowing about this opportunity. Then simply mail off a few of these cards. Don't forget the following:

- family

- friends

- neighbors

- business acquaintances

- the people you buy from

> **note**
> There are estimates that the typical person knows about 800 people in his inner circle.

Telemarketing techniques

Not many people like to sell by using the telephone, but then again there are a lot of people that do. One thing is for sure, a good telemarketing person can quickly sponsor many people in this program for you. If you are comfortable with the telephone, let me show you an easy way to promote this program. If you are not comfortable with the phone, let me show you how to find telemarketing people that you will want to sponsor into your MLM programs.

How to do telemarketing

The trick to telemarketing is to work with referrals. That is, you want to call people that were referred to you. If you call someone and say, "Mr. So-and-So asked me to call you," you can be sure that the person will be cordial and attentive. Compare this approach to the cold calls you get from strangers who try to sell you something out of the blue over the phone. Many direct sales companies depend 100% on using referrals. When they talk to anyone, they always make a habit of asking for referrals. They never run out of good leads since they are constantly generating several referrals with each person that they talk to.

The easiest way to get a few referrals is to ask for them from your "inner warm circle." Simply ask your friends if they know of anyone that would like to earn a few hundred dollars part time by circulating postcards. Another way is to make a few cold calls on the phone. Just pick up the phone and call a few random numbers and say something like this, "Hi, my name is John Doe and I'm looking for a few people in your area that would like to earn some extra money circulating postcards. Do you happen to know of anyone?"

E-Z TIP If you have access to a fax machine, you can FAX hundreds of local business offices. Make up a sheet of paper and write or type a note on it with a copy of the postcard and you're all set.

Once you have 5 or 10 referrals, your cold calls are over. When you call people that were referred to you, you change your sales pitch slightly like this, "Hi, my name is John Doe and Mary Smith mentioned that you may know of some people in your area that would be interested in earning a few extra dollars per month by circulating post cards" (let him answer and take a lot of notes of the people that he is mentioning). Make sure you get their phone numbers. Then say, "In fact, Mary Smith also mentioned that you might be interested?"

When you talk to someone that is interested, tell them that you will send a postcard explaining the offer. And do so. You may then want to follow up in a few days to make sure they send in their order. In summary, develop a few referrals, and then snowball the quantity of referrals with everyone that you talk to. The trick is to ask for the referrals first before you explain the offer.

How to find telemarketers that will help you

I'm sure that you see how a good telemarketer can generate a lot of business for you. If you can find a few telemarketers that you can sponsor into this program, they will quickly sponsor a lot of new people. Consider the following methods:

- ✦ Find out the location of professional telemarketer offices. You can generally find them by looking in the yellow pages. Then go there and place postcards on the windshields in the parking lot.

- ✦ Place a classified advertisement in your local paper. Say something like, "Telemarketers wanted. Work your own hours from home. Call for details." When they call, get their name and address and send them a postcard.

- ✦ Call telemarketing firms. Ask if they are interested in your program on a commission basis. If not, do they know of anyone that might be? (use the referral techniques described above.)

Local advertising techniques

- Place a classified ad for leads. Say something like this, *Part time workers needed for circulating postcards*. When you get a call, send the postcard.

- Sell the plan directly by mail. Advertise this, *65 Easy Ways You Can Make Money Circulating Postcards. Complete Plan—$2.00.*

- Place small space ads in local newspapers. Try the smaller newspapers first. Also, check out the special newspapers that offer advertising that you pay for only when you sell something.

Check with your local ad agencies. Find out if they have any specials that you might consider.

- Use coupon booklets. Most communities have several discount coupon books that are sent by mass mail. Consider these and include the entire postcard copy for this.

Use direct mail locally

Any company or organization that has a lot of members, employees or customers may be interested in making these benefits available to their associates. If you concentrate on companies that are small, you normally can send your postcard directly to the owner. These people are shrewd. If you can show the company owner how you can help his associates while making serious money, the owner may be interested.

If you go to your library, you will find many listings of local organizations that you can mail to. Here are a few to consider:

Service organizations

Any service company that offers monthly service is excellent since they normally send out a bill to their customers. The postcard can be sent postage free. If you have friends or relatives in this kind of business, they may do this for you as a favor. Or, they may be interested in your MLM program and do it themselves. Either way, YOU earn money.

+ cable TV companies

+ contractors

+ plumbers

+ lawn care companies

+ other establishments

+ small manufacturers

+ distributors

note If you sponsor any person who has a lot of contacts, just think how many people he will be able to sponsor.

+ trade organizations. There are many of these organizations. If you can sponsor just one, they may sponsor hundreds or even thousands of new people.

+ unions. What a great opportunity.

+ consumer groups and organizations. Can you imagine how many people you might sponsor through these organizations?

+ fund raising groups. This program is a natural for groups that are soliciting the public in order to raise funds. A lot of these use kids and teenagers that go door to door. What better way to have your postcards circulated. And, the fund raiser clubs or organization can build a residual income just like you are doing. Consider these:

- youth organizations. Locate them in your Yellow Pages or library.

- schools

- churches

Delivery and circulating sources

Many people make a living by delivering their products either to retail outlets or to the consumer. If you sponsor any of these people, they have thousands of locations that they routinely visit and can easily pass out or place postcards. Consider these:

✦ pizza restaurants

✦ chicken restaurants that deliver

✦ newspaper delivery managers

✦ magazine distributors—Wow! This would be just great!

✦ distributors who call on retail outlets

Companies who sell products are always looking for a sales incentive to give away. They use this technique to entice people into their retail establishment, or as a promotional item to give away when the customer buys their product. For example, let's say your local video store has a sign that says, *Rent 3 videos, and get our report: How To Make Money With Postcards . . . . 65 Easy Postage FREE Moneymaking Methods Revealed! FREE!* Get the idea? The video store rents more videos and also builds a downline (and, in the process, your downline, as well). Places to consider are:

- video stores

- book stores

- gift shops

- mail-order dealers—great closing item!

- magazine or newspaper publisher. Can you imagine how many people could be sponsored by a magazine publisher?

- clubs and organization—incentive to join

- any small retail establishment

Use local group advertising

Once you have 10 people in your organization, consider advertising to help your downline. That is, make arrangements with your local newspaper, radio or even TV stations. With 10 people in your immediate downline, the advertising cost can be spread out, making it a reasonable cost per person. Your job is simply to make the arrangements so they can all generate good leads for themselves.

Don't get taken

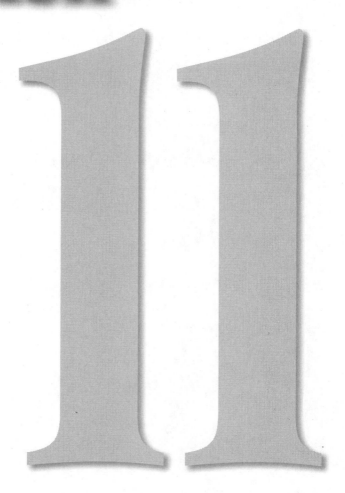

11

Chapter 11

Don't get taken

This review is taken DIRECTLY from a piece of " junk mail." It is the program that starts out with the heading: *Before You Decide To Throw This Away, Please Read the Enclosed At Least Once—Then Decide. This is Not a Chain Letter!*

The first paragraph reads: *I received this program before and threw it away, but later I wondered if I shouldn't have given it a try. Of course, I had no idea who to contact to get a copy, so I had to wait until I was mailed another copy of the program—eleven months later. I DIDN'T throw this one away. I made $41,000 on the first try!* Signed by D. Wilburn, Muncie, IN.

In order to get your attention quick, Mr. or Ms. Wilburn shares the experience of making the mistake of throwing the letter away. A normal person says to themselves, "I don't want to make the same mistake Wilburn did. He had to wait another 11 months before he got a second chance, so I better really read this thing." But, in reality, this piece of junk has floated around for years, and if you miss this copy, you'll get another one tomorrow or the day after.

The next thing you see is a bold headline reading: *You are about to make at least $50,000 in less than 90 days—from the comfort of your own home. Read the enclosed program, then read it again.* Although you may be skeptical, the idea of making money has been planted in your mind—right up front. This will cause you to keep reading a little while longer.

The rest of the page is completely filled with hype—proclaiming that everything is LEGITIMATE and LEGAL. Claims are made that the program works 100% every time and that thousands have used the program to raise capital to start their own business, pay off debts, homes, cars, etc., and even retire. You can ALWAYS recognize a scam because it is based upon a powerful emotional appeal. Think about it. Doesn't everyone on the planet want money to start a business? Pay off debts? Have homes, cars, etc.? Would anyone turn this offer away? NO! That is what makes it so easy to recognize as a scam—they appeal to everybody, yet do nothing! They cruelly play upon your emotions.

Frank T. of Bel Air, MD, offers his personal testimonial at the top of Page 2. Look in the phone book and try to find either D. Wilburn or Frank T. Notice how only partial names and addresses are presented. This is so nobody can find them. But why bother? They don't exist!

The instructions are presented on the rest of Page 2. They consist of precise directions for ordering four products at $5 each and instructions for moving the names around on the list. This is a typical chain letter. Because 99.9% of everyone receiving it replaces their name and members of their family with the people listed, it doesn't work!

These instructions are dumb. Their only purpose is to make you feel as though you are doing something worthwhile. Actually, they are selling you worthless products; products which you may never receive.

Page 3 instructs you to mail the letter you are reading to the names on a mailing list. Of course, when you order the products, you get information on where to purchase this mailing list. Don't you see that these people only care about selling you a mailing list? They could care less if you get a response or not because they already made their money from your purchase of their names and addresses. In fact, you are told to get names and addresses from your phone book. Come on! This is the ABSOLUTE WORST way to sell anything simply because you have no idea what those people would be interested in.

 note Even if you sold a real product, for example baby-sitting services, you wouldn't sit down and advertise by writing letters to everyone in the phone book. Instead, you'd place an ad in the paper and have people interested in baby-sitting contact you.

Now comes the guarantee. It says, *The check point which guarantees your success is simply this: you must receive 15 to 20 orders for Report 1. This is a must. If you don't within two weeks, then send out more programs until you do. Then, a couple weeks later, you should receive at least 100 orders for Report 2.* Notice the word *"should."* The fact is, you could mail constantly and you'll NEVER get 15 to 20 orders. You'd be lucky to get even one. Believe me—thousands of people have put the chain letter theory to a variety of tests and given it every chance in the world to make money. None have ever worked.

CAUTION

Now, here's the hype that really gets most people. Here it is reprinted in its entirety:

Let's say you decide to start small, just to see how it goes, and we will assume you and all those involved send only 200 programs each. Let's also assume that the mailing receives a 5% response. Using a good list, the response could be much better. Also, many people will send thousands of programs instead of 200! But, continuing with this example, you send out 200 programs. With a 5% response, that is, 10 orders for Report 1 (ten people *responded by sending out 200 programs each) for a total of 2,000. The 5% response brings 100 orders for report 2. Those mail out 200 programs for a total of 20,000. The 5% response to those is 1,000 orders for Report 3. The 1,000 send out 200,000 total and the 5% response to that is 10,000 orders for Report 4 (10,000 x $5 for you.) Your total income in this example is $50 + $550 + $5,000 + $50,000 + $55,550. Remember, friend, this is assuming that 95 out of 100 people you mail to will do absolutely nothing and trash this program. Dare to think what would happen if everyone sent 1,000 programs instead of only 200. Believe it, many people will do that and more. By the way, at current prices, your cost to send out 200 programs is less than $100. The participation fee is ridiculously low when you consider what you stand to gain! Consider yourself fortunate to be invited to participate in an exclusive program that really works. Have faith. Think positively, Keep in mind that your investment is minimal and it's easy money invested in you.*

> ⚠️ **CAUTION** Anyone hiding is a scam artist. No doubt about it!

What lies! The truth of the matter is that it really would work if everyone did what they were supposed to do—but they won't. I'll prove it. Go to a crowded place (like a mall). Walk up to the first person you meet and ask them to give you a $5 bill. In return for their $5, they will get $50,000 if they will just find 10,000 other people to give them $5 by promising them the same thing. How many people do you think will take you up on your offer? So, if you couldn't work the program in person, what makes you think it will work through the mail with people who have no idea who you are? The truth is it does not work. It NEVER will!

Page 4 is a personal note from the originator of the program, Edward L. Green. He doesn't list a city and state beside his name. Why? It is because his full name is used. (Remember, nobody wants you to find these people.) A real testifier would be proud to give you his/her full name, full address and phone number so you could get in touch with him/her to find out more about the program.

Edward L Green tells you about how poor he was in 1979. He also says that he will never see a penny of your money. He has already made $4 million and wants to retire. Give me a break. If you made $4 million, wouldn't you want $5 million or $10 million or $20 million? Why stop at a measly $4 million when you could be featured on the *Lifestyles of the Rich and Famous* and be interviewed by Robin Leach?

Amazingly though, on Page 5, Johnson Distributing gives a real name and address. But, try to get their phone number from the address, P.O. Box 7, SAFB IL 42225-0007. It doesn't exist!

Page 6 and 7 contain letters from Chris Johnson, Paul Johnson, A. Zurki, Carl Winslow, A.S. Jalosyk, Bill Nelson, J.T. Adams, Charles Fairchild, Tommy Jayhet, and Mary Rockland. They all tell you some hard luck story about how this program changed their life. Again, try to contact them.

Do you get the picture yet? Almost all scams follow this same general theme. Don't get taken!

Where to place ads that pull like crazy

12

Chapter 12
Where to place ads that pull like crazy

Classified advertising has always been, and will continue to be, the favorite advertising method of mail order "pros." Almost all pros started with tiny inexpensive ads since they represent the most cost effective way to reach millions of people.

Two basic methods

Two basic methods are used with classified advertising. (1) Place an add offering FREE literature, and then send your literature to all inquiries. A free offer will always out-pull an ad that requests money, but your overall profits may be larger because it will generate more inquiries. This method is excellent when you are also collecting "Opportunity Seeker" names that you can rent. You should be able to generate fresh national leads for $.20 to $1 using this method. (2) Offer a report for $2 or $3 and then send out other offers with your orders. This eliminates the "Opportunity Seeker" who never buys anything; your operation is much cleaner and devoid of "busy" work.

Over 200 listed publications

Following is a list of over 200 magazines that offer classified advertising. The first group of magazines represents the favorites of the mail-order pros. These will always out-pull other magazines. The second group has been selected from thousands of other magazines because (1) they offer classified advertising, and (2) they are the least expensive (word cost/circulation ratio). Notice that the last column provides the word cost/circulation ratio. That is, this ratio shows you how much each word will cost for for every 1,000 people who get the magazine. The lower this ratio is, the more cost effective it is. For example, if you were to advertise in the *National Enquirer*, it would cost $8.95 for each word, and it will cost you $.0023 for each 1,000 persons that get the *National Enquirer*. In this example, if you placed a 10-word ad, it will cost you $89.50, and it will be sent out to 3,500,000 people.

Cost/circulation ratios

This may seem like an expensive ad, but the cost to get your 10 word ad to 1,000 people is only ($.0023 x 10) = $.023! That's right—two cents for every 1,000 people! It is important to calculate this circulation/cost ratio to arrive at the relative cost of the ad. As a further example, consider advertising in Hounds and Hunting. Here the cost for a word is only $.22. Good deal? NO! In this case your word cost per 1,000 is $.0227. Therefore, your cost to place a 10 word ad per 1,000 people is ($.0227 x 10) = $.227! That's over 10 times more expensive than the National Enquirer! However, if you were selling something for hunting, it might actually pull better than a general publication.

Ask for rate card

Before you place an ad, write to the magazine and ask for their "rate card" for both classified ads and space advertising. You will normally receive a large package containing a sample publication, advertising rates, schedules and discounts offered for multiple insertions placed for sequential publication dates.

This group of publications have always proven to produce excellent results for opportunity offers:

MAGAZINE NAME	CIRCULATION	
Globe Group P.O. Box 21 Rouses Point, NY 12979-0021	3,000,000	Weekly
The Star P.O. Box 1510 Clearwater, FL 34617	2,900,000	Weekly
National Enquirer P.O. Box 10178 Clearwater, FL 34617	3,500,000	Weekly
Grier's Almanac P.O. Box 888281 Atlanta, GA 30356	3,011,680	Annually
Field & Stream Two Park Ave New York, NY 10016-5695	2,000,000	Monthly
Classified, Inc. 100 E. Ohio Street, Suite 632 Chicago, IL 60611	25,000,000+	Monthly
Grit Stauffer's Magazine Group 1503 S.W. 42nd St. Topeka, KS 66609-1265	330,496	10 times/yr

MAGAZINE NAME	CIRCULATION	
Capper's Stauffer's Magazine Group 1503 S.W. 42nd St. Topeka, KS 66609-1265	353,422	26 times/yr
Popular Science 2 Park Ave. New York, NY 10016	1,861,155	Monthly
Popular Mechanics 224 West 5 Seventh Street New York, NY 10019	1,633,210	Monthly
The Workbasket 700 West 4 Seventh St., Suite 310 Kansas City, MO 64112	2,726,000	6 times/yr
Home Mechanix 2 Park Ave. New York, NY 10016	1,003,244	Monthly
Crafts 'N Things 701 Lee St. #1000 Des Plaines, IL 60016	287,828	8 times/yr
The Family Handyman 28 W. 23rd Street New York, NY 10010	1,000,000	10 times/yr
Workbench 700 West 4 Seventh St., Suite 310 Kansas City, MO 64112	1,025,000	6 times/yr
Crafts Magazine P.O. Box 1790 Peoria, IL 61656	1,000,000	Monthly
Money Making Opportunities 11071 Ventura Blvd. Studio City, CA 91604	222,000	8 times/yr

MAGAZINE NAME	CIRCULATION	
Spare Time Magazine 5810 W. Oklahoma Ave. Milwaukee, WI 53219	301,000	9 times/yr
INC. Magazine 38 Commercial Wharf Boston, MA 02110-3883	647,211	Monthly
Fate Llewellyn Publications Box 64383 St. Paul, MN 55164	200,000	Monthly
Income Opportunities 1500 Broadway, Suite 600 New York, NY 10019	400,000	Monthly
Success PO Box 570 Clearwater, FL 34617-0570	1,200,000	10 times/yr
Book Business Mart Premier Publishers P.O. Box 330309 Fort Worth, TX 76163-0309	50,000	3 times/yr
Opportunity & Income Plus 73 Spring Street #303 New York, NY 10012	250,000	Monthly
Entrepreneur P.O. Box 570 Clearwater, FL 34617-0570	1,700,000	Monthly
Black Enterprise 130 Fifth Ave. New York, NY 10011	240,000	Monthly
Mail Profits P.O. Box 4785 Lincoln, NE 68504	15,000	6 times/yr

Magazines with low cost/circulation ratios

MAGAZINE NAME	CIRCULATION	
Hemmings Motor News P.O. Box 256 Rt 9 West Blvd Bennington, VT 05201	261,551	Monthly
Old Farmers Almanac PO Box 520/Main Street Dublin, NH 03444	4,400,000	Annually
Ladies Birthday Alman. 1715 W. 38th St. Chattanooga, TN 37409	3,803,450	Annually
Cat Fancy 2401 Beverly Blvd. Los Angeles, CA 90057	237,528	Monthly
Antique Trader Weekly P.O. Box 1050 Dubuque, IA 52001	190,000	Weekly
Cars and Parts PO Box 482 911 Vandermark Rd. Sidney, OH 45365	106,111	Monthly
American Rifleman 470 Spring Park Place Herndon, VA 22070	1,372,371	Monthly
American Hunter 470 Spring Park Place Herndon, VA 22070	1,359,643	Monthly
Railfan and Railroad Carsten's Publications, Inc. P.O. Box 700 Newton, NJ 07860	44,216	Monthly

MAGAZINE NAME	CIRCULATION	
Bird Talk P.O. Box 57900 2401 Beverly Blvd. Los Angeles, CA 90057-0900	123,134	Monthly
Model Railroader 1027 N. Seventh St. Milwaukee, WI 53233	181,683	Monthly
Sports Collectors Digest 700 East State St. Iola, WI 54990	43,361	Weekly
Muscle Car Review Dobbs Publishing Group, Inc. 3816 Industry Boulevard Lakeland, FL 33811	71,235	10 times/yr
American Legion Magazine P.O. Box 1055 Indianapolis, IN 46206	3,004,913	Monthly
Crochet World House of White Birches 306 East Parr Rd Berne, IN 46711	72,300	6 times/yr
Gun Week Box 488 Station C Buffalo, NY 14209	20,000+	Weekly
Quiltworld House of White Birches 306 East Parr Rd. Berne, IN 46711	71,000	6 times/yr
Woodman of the World Mag. 1700 Farnam St. Omaha, NE 68102	466,625	Monthly

MAGAZINE NAME	CIRCULATION	
California Senior Citizens 4805 Alta Canyada Road La Canada, CA 91011	69,000	Monthly
Sew News P.O. Box 1790 - News Plaza Peoria, IL 61656	235,000	Monthly
American Motorcyclist 33 Collegeview Road Westerville, OH 43081	176,169	Monthly
American Collector's Journal P.O. Box 407 Kewanee, IL 61443	50,926	Bi-Monthly
Shooting Times News Plaza P.O. Box 1790 Peoria, IL 61656	196,441	Monthly
Dog Fancy 2401q Beverly Blvd. Los Angeles, CA 90057	135,320	Monthly
Guns Magazine Publisher's Development 591 Camino de la Reina, Ste. 200 San Diego, CA 92108	205,619	Monthly
National History 488 Madison Ave. New York, NY 10022	511,463	Monthly
Baseball Digest Trump Card Marketing 222 Cedar Lane Teaneck, NJ 07666	297,490	Monthly
Farm Journal 230 W. Washington Sq. Philadelphia, PA 19106-3599	730,145	13 times/yr

MAGAZINE NAME	CIRCULATION	
The Farmer 1999 Shepard Rd. St. Paul, MN 55116	118,459	21 times/yr
Finescale Modeler 1027 N. Seventh St. Milwaukee, WI 53233	77,748	Bimonthly
Trains 1027 N. Seventh St. Milwaukee, WI 53233	91,749	Monthly
Good Old Days House of White Birches 306 East Parr Rd. Berne, IN 46711	72,500	Monthly
Dune Buggies & Hot VW's 2950-A7 Airway Ave. Costa Mesa, CA 92626	107,302	Monthly
American Handgunner Magazine Publishers Development 591 Camino de la Reina, Ste. 200 San Diego, CA 92108	179,751	6 times/yr
Fur-Fish-Fame 2878 E. Main Street Columbus, OH 43209	172,847	Monthly
Changing Times 1729 H St., N.W. Washington, DC 20006	1,372,867	Monthly
B'nai B'rith Jewish Monthly 823 United Nations Plaza New York, NY 10017	171,457	Monthly
QST 225 Main Street Newington, CT 06111	161,442	Monthly

MAGAZINE NAME	CIRCULATION	
Railroad Model Craftsman Carsten's Publications, Inc. P.O. Box 700 Newton, NJ 07860	72,315	Monthly
Power Boat 15917 Strathern St. Van Nuys, CA 91406	83,224	11 times/yr
Saturday Evening Post 1100 Waterway Blvd. Indianapolis, IN 46202	500,000	6 times/yr
Successful Farming Locust at 1 Seventh St. Des Moines, IA 50336	575,686	14 times/yr
Hunting 8490 Sunset Blvd. Los Angeles, CA 90069	311,715	Monthly
Michigan-Out-Of-Doors 2101 Wood St. Lansing, MI 48912	101,066	Monthly
The Rotarian 1560 Sherman Ave. Evanston, IL 60201	510,000	Monthly
Car and Driver 1515 Broadway New York, NY 10036	900,691	Monthly
Organic Gardening 33 E. Minor St. Emmanus, PA 18098	1,188,335	Monthly
Country Music City News 50 Music Square West, 6th Floor Nashville, TN 37203-3246	500,000	Monthly

MAGAZINE NAME	CIRCULATION	
Bowling 5301 South 76th Street Greendale, WI 53129-0500	131,351	6 times/yr
Motor Trend 8490 Sunset Blvd Los Angeles, CA 90069	738,964	Monthly
Soldiers of Fortune P.O. Box 693 Boulder, CO 80306	105,000	Monthly
W.C.—Cross Stitch 306 East Parr Rd Berne, IN 46711	72,851	Bimonthly
Equus 656 Quince Orchard Rd. Gaithersburg, MD 20878	138,011	Monthly
Our Sunday Visitor 200 Noll Plaza Huntington, IN 46750	115,000	Weekly
W.C.—Home Cooking 306 East Parr Road Berne, IN 46711	68,265	Monthly
Flower and Garden 700 West 4 Seventh . St., Suite 310 Kansas City, MO 64112	4,171,000	6 times/yr
Full Cry Gault Publications P.O. Box 10 Boody, IL 62514	33,955	Monthly
American Cage-Bird Mag. One Glamore Court Smithtown, NY 11787	40,000	Monthly

MAGAZINE NAME	CIRCULATION	
Prorodeo 101 Prorodeo Dr. Colorado Springs, CO 80919	26,567	Bi-weekly
Football Digest Trump Card Marketing 222 Cedar Lane Teaneck, NJ 07666	203,182	10 times/yr
Guns & Ammo 8490 Sunset Blvd. Los Angeles, CA 90063	521,638	Monthly
Modern Photography 825 Seventh Ave. New York, NY 10019	650,386	Monthly
Family Motor Coach Association 8291 Clough Pike Cincinnati, OH 45244	98,000	Monthly
The Highlander P.O. Box 397 Barrington, IL 60011	38,000	7 times /yr
Craft Art Needlework Digest P.O. Box 584 Lake Forest, IL 60045	101,189	Bimonthly
Yankee Yankee Publishing, Inc. 4850 Gaidrew Road Alpharetta, GA 30201	2,900,000	Monthly
National Speed Sport News P.O. Box 608 79 Chestnut Street Ridgewood, NJ 07451-0608	75,000	Weekly
National Review 150 E. 35th Street New York, NY 10016	240,000	25 times/yr

MAGAZINE NAME	CIRCULATION	
Collectors Mart P.O. Box 12830 Wichita, KS 67277	86,623	6 times/yr
Lapidary Journal P.O. Box 80937 San Diego, CA 92138	35,982	Monthly
Easyriders 28210 Dorothy Dr. Agoura Hills, CA 91301	356,590	Monthly
Video Review 902 Broadway New York, NY 10010	450,001	Monthly
Basketball Digest Trump Card Marketing 222 Cedar Lane Teaneck, NJ 07666	104,238	8 times/yr
Winning! Newsletter 5300 City Plex Tower Jenks, OK 74037-5300	100,000	Monthly
Teddy Bear and Friends 900 Fredrick Street Cumberland, MD 21502	60,743	6 times/yr
Women's Circle House of White Birches 306 East Parr Road Berne, IN 46711	49,100	6 times/yr
Shutterbug P.O. Box F Titusville, FL 32781	90,000	Monthly
High Fidelity 825 Seventh Ave. New York, NY 10019	300,172	Monthly

MAGAZINE NAME	CIRCULATION	
Skiing 1515 Broadway New York, NY 10036	440,370	7 times/yr
Soundings 33 Pratt St. Essex, CT 06426	105,606	Monthly
Motorcyclist 8490 Sunset Blvd. Los Angeles, CA 90069	209,757	Monthly
Horoscope 245 Park Ave. New York, NY 10167	104,200	Monthly
Practical Homeowner 33 E. Minor St. Emmaus, PA 18048	708,504	9 times/yr
Bassmaster One Bell Rd. Montgomery, AL 36117	530,757	Monthly
Antique Monthly P.O. Drw. 2 Tuscaloosa, AL 35402	66,243	Monthly
Pipe Smoker P.O. Box 22085 Chattanooga, TN 37422	25,000	Monthly
Banana Republic Trips Mag. One Harrison St. San Francisco, CA 94105	300,000	Monthly
Camping & RV Magazine P.O. Box 337 Iola, WI 54945	20,000	Monthly

MAGAZINE NAME	CIRCULATION	
Women's Household House of White Birches 306 East Parr Road Berne, IN 46711	39,200	Quarterly
Body, Mind & Spirit P.O. Box 701 Providence, RI 02401	152,000	Monthly
Cycle 1515 Broadway New York, NY 10036	373,398	Monthly
Today's Chicago Woman 200-West Superior, #400 Chicago, IL 60610	125,000	Monthly
Lottery Player's Magazine 321 New Albany Rd. Moorestown, NJ 08057	180,127	Monthly
Video 460 W. 34th St New York, NY 10001	407,050	Monthly
Archery 319 Barry Ave. Suite 101 Wayzata, MN 55391	113,023	Monthly
Quarter Horse Journal 2701 I-40 East P.O. Box 200 Amarillo, TX 79168	67,664	Monthly
W.C.—Country Needlecraft 306 East Parr Rd. Berne, IN 46711	44,508	Monthly
Modern Drummer 870 Pomton Ave. Cedar Grove, NJ 07009	78,400	Monthly

MAGAZINE NAME	CIRCULATION	
International Travel News 2120 28th St. Sacramento, CA 95818	26,109	Monthly
Worldradio 2120 28th St. Sacramento, CA 95818	25,833	Monthly
Kiwanis 3636 Woodview Trace Indianapolis, IN 46268	279,249	Monthly
Power and Motoryacht 1234 Summer St. Stamford, CT 06905	135,319	Monthly
Modern Electronics 76 N. Broadway Hicksville, NY 11801	75,241	Monthly
Sail 100 First Ave Charlestown, MA 02129	175,212	Monthly
The Lutheran 426 S. Fifth Ave. Minneapolis, MN 55448	1,083,181	Monthly
Americana 29 W. 38th St. New York, NY 10018	325,186	Monthly
Horse Trader P.O. Box 728 Middlefield, OH 44062	28,370	Monthly
Passenger Train Journal P.O. Box 6128 Glendale, CA 91205	16,151	Monthly

MAGAZINE NAME	**CIRCULATION**	
Runner's World 33 E. Minor St. Emmaus, PA 18049	451,512	Monthly
The Log P.O. Box 89309 San Diego, CA 92318	46,960	Monthly
Harvard Magazine 7 Ware St. Cambridge, MA 02138	186,677	Monthly
Horse Illustrated 25025 I-45 North, Suite 390 Spring, TX 77380	135,609	Monthly
Trailer Boats 20700 Belshaw Ave. Carson, CA 90746	72,501	Monthly
Skip P.O. Box 404 Bala Cynwyd, PA 19004	35,400	Monthly
Trailblazer 15375 S.E. 30th Place Bellevue, WA 98007	94,572	Monthly
Saltwater Sportsman 186 Lincoln St. Boston, MA 02111	128,521	Monthly
Midwest Outdoors 111 Shore Dr. Burr Ridge, IL 60521	37,773	Monthly
Golf 380 Madison Ave. New York, NY 10017	912,157	Monthly

MAGAZINE NAME	CIRCULATION	
Southern Outdoors P.O. Box 17915 Montgomery, AL 36141	288,963	Monthly
Cats Magazine 445 Merrimac Dr. Port Orange, FL 32019	129,332	Monthly
Western Horseman 3850 N. Nevada Ave. Colorado Springs, CO 80933	162,369	Monthly
Guitar World 1115 Broadway New York, NY 10010	128,823	Monthly
Mother Jones 1633 Misson St. San Francisco, CA 94103	183,864	Monthly
Flying Models Box 700 Newtown, NJ 07860	27,073	Monthly
Golf Digest 5520 Park Ave. Trumbull, CT 06611	1,239,100	Monthly
Fishing World 700 West 4 Seventh St., Suite 310 Kansas City, MO 64112	341,215	6 times/yr
Christian Herald 40 Overlook Dr. Chappaqua, NY 10514	142,376	Monthly
UCLA Monthly 1633 Westwood Blvd., Ste 110 Los Angeles, CA 90024	186,000	Monthly

MAGAZINE NAME	CIRCULATION	
Video Marketplace 990 Grove St. Evanston, IL 60201	140,000	Monthly
Owner Builder 1516 Fifth St. Berkeley, CA 94710	66,150	Monthly
Pennsylvania Sportsman P.O. Box 5196 Harrisburg, PA 17110	65,490	Monthly
Woodenboat P.O. Box 78 Brooklyn, ME 04616	103,180	Monthly
Ensign P.O. Box 31664 Raleigh, NC 27622	54,534	Monthly
Small Boat Journal Box 400 Bennington, VT 05201	57,103	Monthly
Women's Sports and Fitness 809 S. Orlando Ave., Ste H Winter Park, FL 32789	300,708	Monthly
Dirt Bike 10600 Sepulveda Blvd. Mission Hills, CA 91345	131,930	Monthly
True West P.O. Box 2107 Stillwater, OK 74076	32,939	Monthly
Jazz Times 8055 13th St., Suite 301 Silver Springs, MD 20910	49,237	Monthly

MAGAZINE NAME	CIRCULATION	
Tours & Resorts 990 Grove St. Evanston, IL 60201	194,716	Monthly
Hockey Digest Trump Card Marketing 222 Cedar Lane Teaneck, NJ 07666	103,506	Monthly
Canoe P.O. Box 3146 Kirkland, WA 98083	64,060	Monthly
The Nation 72 5th Ave New York, NY 10011	79,978	Monthly
World Tennis 3 Park Ave. New York, NY 10016	383,059	Monthly
BackStretch 19363 James Couzens Hwy. Detroit, MI 48235	25,380	Monthly
Motor Boating and Sailing 224 W. 5 Seventh St. New York, NY 10019	141,463	Monthly
Car Collector/Car Classics P.O. Box 28571 Atlanta, GA 30328	31,318	Monthly
Circus 3 West 18th St. New York, NY 10011	281,842	Monthly
National Lampoon 155 Avenue of the Americas New York, NY 10013	250,002	Monthly
Total Health 6001 Topanga Canyon Rd. Woodland Hills, CA 91367	71,010	Monthly

MAGAZINE NAME	CIRCULATION	
Bestways P.O. Box 2028 Carson City, NV 89702	161,815	Monthly
Writer's Digest 1507 Dana Ave. Cincinnati, OH 45207	220,196	Monthly
Boating 1515 Broadway New York, NY 10036	188,057	Monthly
Horticulture 20 Park Plaza, Suite 1220 Boston, MA 02116	178,508	Monthly
New Age 342 Western Ave. Brighton, MA 02135	151,730	Monthly
N.J. Hunting and Fishing P.O. Box 100 Somerdale, NJ 08083	15,000	Monthly
Dog World 29 North Wacker Dr. Chicago, IL 60606	64,732	Monthly
Outdoor America 1701 N. Ft. Meyer Dr. Arlington, VA 22209	43,422	Monthly
Sport Fishing 809 South Orlando Ave. Winter Park, FL 32789	109,384	Monthly
Old West P.O. Box 2107 Stillwater, OK 74076	28,385	Monthly
Treasure 6745 Adobe Rd. 29 Palms, CA 92277	22,679	Monthly

MAGAZINE NAME	CIRCULATION	
Petersen's Photo Magazine 8490 Sunset Blvd. Los Angeles, CA 90069	283,010	Monthly
Fine Woodworking P.O. Box 355 Newtown, CT 06470	296,773	Monthly
Old House Journal 69th & Seventh Ave. Brooklyn, NY 11217	97,948	6 times/yr
Snowmobile 319 Barry Ave.S., Suite 101 Wayzata, MN 55391	419,478	Monthly
Lost Treasure P.O. Box 937 Bixby, OK 74008	41,423	Monthly
Cycle News 2201 Cherry Ave. Long Beach, CA 90806	60,700	Monthly
Yachting 1515 Broadway New York, NY 10036	136,028	Monthly
N.Y. Review of Books 250 E. 5 Seventh St. New York, NY 10107	114,234	Monthly
American Film 3. E. 54th St. New York, NY 10022	133,232	Monthly
Pure-Bred Dogs Amer. Kennel 51 Madison Ave. New York, NY 10010	53,950	Monthly
Knitting Digest House of White Birches 306 East Parr Rd. Berne, IN 46711	25,600	6 times/yr

MAGAZINE NAME	CIRCULATION	
American Photographer 1515 Broadway New York, NY 10036	254,107	Monthly
Saturday Review 214 Massachusetts Ave. N.E. Washington, DC 20002	200,000	Monthly
Human Events 422 First St. S.E. Waashington, DC 20037	36,695	Monthly
American Business 1775 Broadway New York, NY 10019	104,772	Monthly
Classic Toy Trains 11027 North Seventh St. Milwaukee, WI 53233	10,000	Monthly
Auto Racing Digest Trump Card Marketing 222 Cedar Lane Teaneck, NJ 07666	44,124	Monthly
Soccer Digest Trump Card Marketing 222 Cedar Lane Teaneck, NJ 07666	27,929	Monthly
High Technology Business 214 Lewis Wharf Boston, MA 02110	203,678	Monthly
Western Boatman 20700 Belshaw Ave. Carson, CA 90746	23,961	Monthly
Archaeology 15 Park Row New York, NY 10038	105,146	Monthly

MAGAZINE NAME	CIRCULATION	
Motorcross Action 10600 Sepulveda Blvd. Mission Hills, CA 91345	92,257	Monthly
Threads P.O. Box 355/63 S. Main St. Newtown, CT 06470	125,913	Monthly
UTNE Reader 2732 West 43rd St. Minneapolis, MN 55410	67,449	Monthly
Yoga Journal 2054 University Ave. Berkley, CA 94704	44,819	Monthly
Practical Horseman Gum Tree Corner Unionville, PA 19375	55,752	Monthly
Dirt Wheels 10600 Sepulveda Blvd. Mission Hills, CA 91345	88,632	Monthly
Hounds and Hunting Box 372 Bradford, PA 16701	9,697	Monthly
Backpacker 1515 Broadway New York, NY 10036	172,111	Monthly
Bowling Digest Trump Card Marketing 222 Cedar Lane Teaneck, NJ 07666	104,159	Monthly
Darkroom Photography 9021 Melrose Ave. Los Angeles, CA 90069	70,508	8 times/yr
Miniature Collector 170 5th Ave. New York, NY 10010	23,602	Quarterly

MAGAZINE NAME	CIRCULATION	
Gun Dog 1901 Bell Ave., Suite 4 Des Moines, IA 50315	62,973	Bimonthly
Blums Farmers Almanac 3301 Healy Dr. S.W. Winston-Salem, NC 27103	100,000	Annually
Magazine Antiques 980 Madison Ave. New York, NY 10021	60,578	Monthly
Hispanic Business 360 S. Hope Ave., Suite C. Santa Barbara, CA 93105	107,875	Monthly
Linn's Stamp News P.O. Box 29 Sidney, OH 45365	74,082	Weekly
Selling P.O. Box 570 Clearwater, FL 34617-9862	100,000	Quarterly
Mustang Monthly Dobbs Publishing Group, Inc. 3816 Industry Boulevard Lakeland, FL 33811		Monthly
Super Ford Dobbs Publishing Group, Inc. 3816 Industry Boulevard Lakeland, FL 33811		Monthly
Corvette Fever Dobbs Publishing Group, Inc. 3816 Industry Boulevard Lakeland, FL 33811		Monthly
Mopar Muscle Dobbs Publishing Group, Inc. 3816 Industry Boulevard Lakeland, FL 33811		6 times/yr

Where to place your 1" ads for less than $5.00

NOTE: These prices were accurate as of the publication date, but you should write the publications you are interested in advertising with and get their latest circulation/pricing information.

Publication/Address/Publisher	$Cost/circ.	Circ	Cost/inch
Awesome Adsheet Box 4916, Panorama City CA 91412 Exciting World	3.00	10,000	0.0003
Buy-Sell Opportunities Box 201406, Bloomington MN 55420 Dave Meyers	2.00	5,000	0.0004
New Dawn Technology 8392 Yorkshire, Anaheim CA 92804	6.00	15,000	0.0004
52 Weeks 6006 Greenbelt Rd., Greenbelt MD 20770 Richard Kind	12.00	26,000	0.0005
Atlanta Adsheet 2980 Delmar Ln., Atlanta GA 30311 Lisa Lamb	1.00	2,000	0.0005
Peoples' Advertiser 91 Ames St, Boston MA 02124 Stewart Enterp.	4.00	8,000	0.0005

Publication/Address/Publisher	$Cost/circ.	Circ	Cost/inch
$1 Per Inch Adv. 8581 Twana Dr., Garden Grove, CA 92641 Dick Swan	1.00	2,000	0.0005
Christian M.O. Digest P.O. Box 427, Riva, MD 21140 Ray Goff	3.00	5,000	0.0006
Limelight P.O. Box 249, Quincy IL 62306 J&M Enterprises	3.00	5,000	0.0006
Mario's Crystal Adv. P.O. Box 456, Cranford NJ 07016 Mario Borsellino	6.00	10,000	0.0006
Janet's Ads P.O. Box 226, Vanceboro NC 28586 Janet's Products	2.00	3,000	0.0007
Wise Owl Ads P.O. Box 29422, Baltimore MD 21213 S.O. Jolly	2.00	3,000	0.0007
"Ad"-Venture 35 Edgewood Rd., Portland CT 06480 C.E. McNiff	2.00	3,000	0.0007
Dutch Treat 2985 Bronco Ln., Norco CA 91760 Anne Marieke	7.00	10,000	0.0007

Publication/Address/Publisher	$Cost/circ.	Circ	Cost/inch
Ed Canty's Carolinian Ad 4828 Zorich Dr., Charlotte NC 28227 Ed Canty	7.50	10,000	0.0008
Entrepreneur's Digest P.O. Box 3224, Oshkosh WI 54904	9.00	12,000	0.0008
Thru the Looking Glass P.O. Box 467, Shillington PA 19607 Image Marketing	12.00	16,000	0.0008
Torontos Success Ad 706 Ridge Rd. W., Grimsby On L3M4E7 Success Strategies	15.00	20,000	0.0008
Laurie's Ads 1425 Stabler Ln., Yuba City CA 95991 Laurie J. Wright	8.00	10,000	0.0008
Northern Lights Ad 117 W Harrison, Chicago IL 60605 Dan Beckett	20.00	25,000	0.0008
Tami & Joseph's MO Mkt Box 154, Lincoln City OR 97367 Vita	8.00	10,000	0.0008
The Int's Small Bus Ad 51578 Ond St., South Bend IN 46637 Wiffletree Ind.	12.00	15,000	0.0008
The Wizard of Adz 807 Broadway, Quincy IL 62301 J&M Enterprizes	8.00	10,000	0.0008

Publication/Address/Publisher	$Cost/circ.	Circ	Cost/inch
Toronto's Success Adv 1640 Bayview Ave., Toronto On M4G4E9 Success Strategies	8.00	10,000	0.0008
Calif High Sierra 2615MO N Central Ave., Visalia CA 93291 Calif High Sierra	6.00	7,000	0.0009
Excel Adv 975 Denmore St. NW, Palm Bay FL 132907 Roger Coulther	6.00	7,000	0.0009
Mail Order Messenger P.O. Box 17131, Memphis TN 38187	9.00	10,000	0.0009
The Gleaner Adsheet 6429 Gilson Ave., N Hollywood, CA 91606 Ana Angelescu	2.00	2,200	0.0009
Ben Frank's Almanac Box 655, Pinellas Park FL 34664 Kelly Publ.	12.00	13,000	0.0009
Choice Opportunities Box 600927, N. Miami Bch. FL 33160 Gibbs Publ	6.00	6,000	0.0010
Country Wide Ads Box 270421, Okla City OK 73127 Graham's	2.00	2,000	0.0010
Covert's Adv 14 E 900 N., Layton UT 84041 J.L. Covert	10.00	10,000	0.0010

Publication/Address/Publisher	$Cost/circ.	Circ	Cost/inch
Dale's Rapid Flyer P.O. Box 361, Yuba City CA 95992 D.R. Ford	1.00	1,000	0.0010
Dollar Daze Adv. P.O Box 213, Greenwood NC 29648 Bibb Jones	1.00	1,000	0.0010
Econo Adsheet 146-15 133rd Ave., Jamaica NY 11436 Wm.H. Fordham	2.00	2,000	0.0010
Fast Start Team Adv P.O. Box 70268, Salt Lake City UT 84170 George Norr	5.00	5,000	0.0010
Geneva's Ad-Sheet Rt 1, Box 630, Marble Hill MO 63764 Geneva Strosnider	1.00	1,000	0.0010
Grace's Ad Sheet Rt 2, Box 794, Union Grove AL 3 5175 Grace's	1.50	1,500	0.0010
Graphic Impressions RR1, Box 12, Ararat NC 27007 Graphic Impress.	2.50	2,500	0.0010
Hobbyists & Collectors P.O. Box 1051, Quincy IL 62306 Clarance Gale	5.00	5,000	0.0010

Publication/Address/Publisher	$Cost/circ.	Circ	Cost/inch
Mail Order Adv. 142 Pond St., Wakefield RI 02880 T.F. Holland	2.00	2,000	0.0010
Mailorder Un-Classified P.O Box 402, Clay Center KS 67432 Rice Publ.	3.00	3,000	0.0010
Mail-Courier Express P.O Box 1505, Richmond CA 94802 Andre Gilliam	5.00	5,000	0.0010
Many Happy Returns 6702 Silver Sage, Ft. Worth TX 76137 Pat Catanesi	3.00	3,000	0.0010
Matco Advertiser 415 E Ford Ave., Baltimore MD 21230 Matco Enterp.	2.00	2,000	0.0010
Mighty P.O. or Adsheet 2615 N Central Ave., Visalia CA 93291 Calif. Adsheets	1.00	1,000	0.0010
MO CA Hobby Adsheet 2615 N Central Ave., Visalia CA 93291 Calif. Adsheets	3.00	3,000	0.0010
Money Making Adv P.O Box 600927, N. Miami Bch FL 33160 Gibbs Publ	4.00	4,000	0.0010

Publication/Address/Publisher	$Cost/circ.	Circ	Cost/inch
Northeastern Herald 270 Saratoga Rd. Plaza, Glenville NY 12302 J.L.C. Future Pub	2.00	2,000	0.0010
Ozark Flyer Box 624, Cherokee Village AR 72525 K. Weiland	1.00	1,000	0.0010
Patsy's Gettin' Place Box 106, Carson TX 75636 Patsy Martin	2.00	2,000	0.0010
Rosebud Adsheet 2091 NW 21st Terr. #7-107, Stuart, FL 34994 Andrea Lotak	1.00	1,000	0.0010
Second Income Ntwk. Box 1382, Alameda CA 94501 Ray Thomas	5.00	5,000	0.0010
Sun Coast Adv P.O. Box 17672, Tampa FL 33682 Terry Baker	1.00	1,000	0.0010
Target Advertiser 9078 Eglise Ave, Downey CA 90240 Thms Mongeon	2.00	2,000	0.0010
The Happy House Adv P.O Box 414, Altus AR 72821 Peter Rothe	3.00	3,000	0.0010

Publication/Address/Publisher	$Cost/circ.	Circ	Cost/inch
The Leader P.O Box 27, Lawrenceburg KY 40342 The Leader	5.00	5,000	0.0010
The Leap Ahead Adsheet 1019 Utau Ave, Libby MT 59923 Bonnie J. Wood	2.00	2,000	0.0010
The Mailorder Jungles Ad P.O Box 5521, Stockton CA 95205 P. Lyons & Assoc.	5.00	5,000	0.0010
Today's Riches 21854 North Dr., Nuevo CA 92367 Riches	2.00	2,000	0.0010
Unicorn Express 8640 Guilford Rd., Columbia MD 21046 Kevin O'Rourke	2.00	2,000	0.0010
Mary's Mail Mart Box 60, Albert City IA 50510 M.C. Holt	5.00	4,500	0.0011
Buckeye Bulletin P.O. Box 1188, Fremont OH 43420 Roger Goad Pntg	3.00	2,500	0.0012
Carver Country 36 Indian St., S. Carver MA 02366 N. Malinowski	6.00	5,000	0.0012
Flamingo Advertiser 9122 S. Fed. Hwy 173, Port St. Lucie FL 4952 Andrea Lotak	6.00	5,000	0.0012

Publication/Address/Publisher	$Cost/circ.	Circ	Cost/inch
Idea Digest P.O Box 80, Foyil OK 74031 GD Services	9.00	7,500	0.0012
Mailorder Dynamite P.O. Box 681519, Miami FL 33168 TNT Books	6.00	5,000	0.0012
MO Business Booster Box 309, McKees Port PA 15134 Mark McClellan	6.00	5,000	0.0012
The Kitchen Table Adsh P.O. Box 190, Ridge NY 11961 Peter A. Wigger	6.00	5,000	0.0012
The Silver Sheet P.O. Box 776, Park Ridge IL 60068 R&Z Publ.	6.00	5,000	0.0012
Success Advertiser 2067 S. Linden Ave., Springfield MO 65804 W.G. Smith,	5.00	4,000	0.0013
The Big Ad-Sheet P.O. Box 3087, Jekyll Island GA 31520 Profit Gens	10.00	8,000	0.0013
California Adsheet 2615 N. Central Ave., Visalia, GA 93291 Calif. Adsheets	2.00	1,500	0.0013

Publication/Address/Publisher	$Cost/circ.	Circ	Cost/inch
Christmas Journal P.O. Box 354, Christmas FL 32709 Bob Constable	4.00	3,000	0.0013
Image 6702 Silver Sage, Ft. Worth TX 76137 Pat Catanesi	2.00	1,500	0.0013
Jeanne's MO Clipboard P.O. Box 424, Morganville NJ 07751 Joe Reinbold	4.00	3,000	0.0013
Life Line Rt 1, Box 153, Knob Noster, MO 65336 Joe Patillo	4.00	3,000	0.0013
Phoenix MO Ads & Opp P.O. Box 9762, Baltimore MD 21284 Tom Suit	4.00	3,000	0.0013
Spg Valley Advertiser Rt 1, Box187, W. Baden IN 47469 DMC Publ.	4.00	3,000	0.0013
Superior M.O. Adv. 17047 Gothic Ave, Granada Hills CA 91344 Superior Services	2.00	1,500	0.0013
The Hurricane Fleet 4808 S. Ocean Blvd., Myrtle Beach SC 29575 John Carpenter	4.00	3,000	0.0013

Publication/Address/Publisher	$Cost/circ.	Circ	Cost/inch
Town & Country Adv. P.O. Box 212, Shelbyville TX 75973 Southern Svc. Co	4.00	3,000	0.0013
Whirl Wind Adv. 5375 SW 40th Ave. #205, Ft. Lauderdle. FL 33314 W.J. Weir	2.00	1,500	0.0013
The Chesapeake Adsheet 1511 N. Broadway, Baltimore, MD 21213 R. Dandridge	7.00	5,000	0.0014
Ultimate Advertiser 2024 Sullivan Trail, Easton PA 18042 Eric Snyder	7.00	5,000	0.0014
Baldy's Big Bend Adv. P.O Box 20194, Tallahassee FL 32316 Harry Pinson	2.00	1,400	0.0014
Carolina Trade Winds 522 North, McClure PA 17841 Rhonda Wagner	5.00	3,500	0.0014
Mailorder Fantasia 522 North, McClure PA 17841 Worldwide Ind.	8.00	5,500	0.0015
Ad Affair P.O Box 6782, Orange CA 92613 Sundance Accept	3.00	2,000	0.0015
Calif Mail Gazette Box 508, Duarte CA 91009 Gold Service	6.00	4,000	0.0015

Publication/Address/Publisher	$Cost/circ.	Circ	Cost/inch
Direct Mail Business P.O. Box 1343, Lake Worth FL 33460 Broadway Publ.	15.00	10,000	0.0015
Dir. of Opportunities Rt 1, Box 10790, Madisonville TN 37354 William Lee	6.00	4,000	0.0015
Ray's Business Builder 348 Puuhale Rd., Honolulu HI 96819 Fay & Jim Hoilien	3.00	2,000	0.0015
Home Business P.O. Box 1922, Sumas WA 98295 Home Business	3.00	2,000	0.0015
Little Cheaper Peeper P.O. Box 115, Clinton TN 37717 HTM Subsidiaries	3.00	2,000	0.0015
Mail Ideas Plus Adsheet 319 W. Norris St., Philadelphia PA 19122 MS Mart	3.00	2,000	0.0015
Mailorder Treasure 1741 S. Horne St., Oceanside, CA 92054 United	3.00	2,000	0.0015
One World Advertiser P.O. Box 66164, Albany NY 12206 Lumal Mktg Gp	3.00	2,000	0.0015
Darrel Scheiske 288 Kennendale, TX 76060	4.00	2,000	0.0020

Publication/Address/Publisher	$Cost/circ.	Circ	Cost/inch
Plain-O Ads from Plano 3316 Kingsbridge Dr., Plano TX 75075 Gwen-Franklin	2.00	1,000	0.0020
Pony Express Adv. 12533 Pony Express, Knoxville TN 37922 E. Martin	2.00	1,000	0.0020
Printstop Sales Puller 5406 E. 4th Plain Blvd., Vancouver WA 98661 Printstop	2.00	1,000	0.0020
Profit Pack Marketing P.O. Box 279, Grover NC 28073 Dale Advertising	2.00	1,000	0.0020
Randy's Adsheet 504-A North Seventh St., Las Vegas NV 89101 R.J. Bleicher	2.00	1,000	0.0020
Redwood Record 245 MT. Hermon Rd., Scotts Valley CA 95066 Wealth Wise Pb.	2.00	1,000	0.0020
Road Runner Express P.O. Box 42683, Tucson AZ 85733 Double L Books	2.00	1,000	0.0020
Rogue Ads P.O. Box 115, Gold Bch. OR 97444 L & D Enterprises	2.00	1,000	0.0020

Publication/Address/Publisher	$Cost/circ.	Circ	Cost/inch
R.L.H. Discount Adv.			
P.O Box 331, Mt. Morris, MT 48458	4.00	2,000	0.0020
R.L.H Network D			
Sandlapper			
P.O Box 400, Williamston SC 29697	10.00	5,000	0.0020
Danny Chasteen			
Shirley's Swappers Guide			
P.O Box 346, Drayton SC 29333	2.00	1,000	0.0020
Faith Gift Shop			
Silva's Adsheets			
316 W 51st, New York NY 10019	2.00	1,000	0.0020
Silva Publ.			
Sonlight Advertiser			
P.O Box 469, Bunn NC 27508	2.00	1,000	0.0020
Sonlight			
Special Edition			
Box 4456, Hamilton On L8V4S7	2.00	1,000	0.0020
Niagara Promot.			
Speedy Kads			
P.O Box 270421, Okla. City OK 73127	2.00	1,000	0.0020
Hal Graham			
SRNL Advertiser			
P.O Box 386, Naples NC 28760	2.00	1,000	0.0020
SRNL Advertiser			

Publication/Address/Publisher	$Cost/circ.	Circ	Cost/inch
St. Pete's Ads. P.O. Box 11656 St., Petersburg FL 33733 The Steward CO.	2.00	1,000	0.0020
Sunset Bulletin P.O. Box 187, Oshawa On L1H7L1 Sunset Entp.	2.00	1,000	0.0020
Super Saver Ads 106 Jackson, Knoxville,TN 61448 Nesslser Press	6.00	3,000	0.0020
Supermail P.O. Box 4872, Greenville SC2 9680 James Childers	3.00	1,500	0.0020
Survine's Servant Ads 2365 Oswego, Aurora CO 80010 Survine's	2.00	1,000	0.0020
Sylvia's Legs' 36 Chestnut St., Glen Cove NY 11542 Cedric Naude	6.00	3,000	0.0020
Tammy's Mailbag Adv. P.O. Box 723, Palo Cedro CO 96073 Hartman Entp.	6.00	3,000	0.0020
Texas Star P.O. Box 769, Freeport TX 77541 H & H Enterp.	2.00	1,000	0.0020

Publication/Address/Publisher	$Cost/circ.	Circ	Cost/inch
The Ad Net Express 1202 Ferndale Dr., Round Rock TX 78664 Christy Publ.	2.00	1,000	0.0020
The Best Deal Adv. 16460 Monterey St., Lake Elsinore CA 92530 T. Mongeon	2.00	1,000	0.0020
The Blue Star 1425 Stabler Lane #11, Yuba City CA 95993 Laurie Wright	4.00	2,000	0.0020
The Businessman P.O. Box 0281, Citrus Heights CA 95611 Wright Entp.	2.00	1,000	0.0020
The Canadian Connection Box 4456, Hamilton On L8V4S7 Niagara Promot.	2.00	1,000	0.0020
The Candies Express P.O. Box2241, Batesville, AR 72503 E & S Marketing	4.00	2,000	0.0020
The Clintonian P.O Box 20529, El Cajon CA 92021 Anne L Clinton	2.00	1,000	0.0020
The Early Bird Box 1215, Broderick CA 95605 Easy Street	2.00	1,000	0.0020

Publication/Address/Publisher	$Cost/circ.	Circ	Cost/inch
The Gad About Gazette P.O. Box 602, Merrimack NH 03054 J.E. Leblanc	2.00	1,000	0.0020
The Green Country Adv P.O. Box 1869, Tahlequah OK 74465 Marketing Conc.	2.00	1,000	0.0020
The Green River Adv. P.O Box 93, Greensbury KY 42743 Robert A Judd	3.00	1,500	0.0020
The Lone Star P.O. Box 610473, Port Huron MI 48061 O.J. Primeaux	3.00	1,500	0.0020
The Lynx Advertiser 5723 10th Ave., Los Angeles CA 90043 Tina A. Smith	2.00	1,000	0.0020
The Pay Day Adsheet P.O Box 792, Woodbine NJ 08270 Pay Day Enterp	2.00	1,000	0.0020
Truth in Advertising 2460 Eglinton Ave. E., Scarborough On M1K5J7 MO Dealers Un.	3.00	1,500	0.0020
Wheat State Adv. Route 2, Box 5AA, Larned KS 67550 Florine Seachris	2.00	1,000	0.0020

Publication/Address/Publisher	$Cost/circ.	Circ	Cost/inch
WPB Advertiser 6348 W. 95th St., Oak Lawn IL 60453 Wesley Pntg.	2.00	1,000	0.0020
Zebra Express 81 S Judson St., Gloversville NY 12078 John Marlitt	4.00	2,000	0.0020
$2Bucks-N-Inch Adv. Box 2285, Irwindale CA 91706 Nadco	2.00	1,000	0.0020
The World of Mail Order P.O. Box 3087, Jekyll Island GA 31520	7.00	3,000	0.0023
Willie's Advertiser 4811 16th Ave., Chattanooga TN 37407 W.P. Thrailkill	7.00	3,000	0.0023
Cactus Courier Box 17813, Fountain Hills, AZ 85269 R&S Publ	6.00	2,500	0.0024
Atomic Adlets 807 Broadway #4, Quincy IL 62301 J&M Entp.	5.00	2,000	0.0025
Bucks Adlet P.O Box 270421, Okla. City OK 73127 Hal Graham	5.00	2,000	0.0025
C-More 4915 Lotus Ave., St. Louis MO 63113 W.G. Walker	5.00	2,000	0.0025

Publication/Address/Publisher	$Cost/circ.	Circ	Cost/inch
Golden Advertiser Box 1818, Innisfail AB T0M1A0 Neil Granlund	5.00	2,000	0.0025
Lady Bug Flyer P.O Box 495, Rockville CT 06066 P.G. Aldrich	5.00	2,000	0.0025
New Market Reports 1019 Old Monrovia Rd., Huntsville AL 35806 Patco Mktg.	2.50	1,000	0.0025
Portland Rose 602 NE Church, Portland OR 97211 Pacific Star Pub.	3.00	1,200	0.0025

The most exciting MLM opportuni-ties

13

Chapter 13

The most exciting MLM opportunities

In this chapter are descriptions of many mail-order dealerships that you can buy and promote to earn a handsome profit. There is no inventory required. Most dealerships listed allow you to purchase the program and resell it to others. Most of these dealerships offer additional opportunities for you such as selling books, name lists, etc. Therefore, you have the opportunity to learn the mail order business while earning a profit and generating FREE MLM leads!

If you want more information for a specific dealership offering, send a SASE (self-addressed stamped envelope) plus one loose stamp along with a copy of the description in this chapter to the company's name indicated. If you are requesting details for more than one company from the same source, only one SASE is necessary, but send one loose stamp for each inquiry.

Highly recommended mail-order dealerships and associations

✦ Sell books, manuals & reports, new release program. Keep $20.00 profit on every $25.00 order. With this program, you can start and operate your own thriving mail order information business on a shoestring. Selling the RIGHT TYPE of information is practically a depression-proof business . . . at any time, and you are shown how to sell all type of in-demand reports, books, manuals, courses, etc.

This mail-order program provides a complete dealership and a master dealership with many outstanding benefits. You may become a distributor in this program for $25.00 or send a SASE + 1 loose stamp for complete details to: Videx, Box 1664, Stow, Ohio 44224

✦ Totally Awesome Typesetting & Ad Design Plus Dealership—Earn 50% on ads & $10.00 on brokerships. For details and circular, send SASE plus one loose stamp to: Videx, Box 1664 ,Stow, Ohio 44224

✦ Join the International Mail Dealers' Council. Join the IMDC now for only $30.00 and you receive "The Beginner's Mail Order Kit" valued at $15.00. You get 12 benefits by joining this council plus you earn $10.00 for each member you recruit! Send SASE plus one loose stamp for details to: Videx, Box 1664, Stow, Ohio 44224

✦ Sell high quality mailing lists. These are peel and stick labels you can use for yourself or sell to others. Unlike lists offered by some other companies, these names are updated regularly. Postal Service's National Change of Address file and a national database are used to keep name lists clean. They will replace each undeliverable with 10 fresh names. Choose from many categories such as Opportunity Seekers, Buyer Names, Financial Names and Multi-level Names. Prices are very competitive such as 1,000 names for $50.00. Dealers may rent these names to others for personal use at 50% of normal list price. Bonus:

Receive $10.00 for registering new dealers. Send SASE plus one loose stamp for circular to: Videx, Box 1664, Stow, Ohio 44224

✦ Join the U.S. Team—a discount advertising program for over 80 mail order and MLM publications. For $50.00, you can reach approximately 500,000 potential customers at a 40% discount. This established ad agency will place your ads at 40% discount, and you can promote this program and earn $30.00 for each new member you recruit. Send SASE plus one loose stamp for details to: Videx, Box 1664, Stow, Ohio 44224

✦ How to Become Wealthy as a circular mailer. This publication describes many ways of making money from home by mailing circulars based on the publishers many years of experience. A dealership offer for promoting this program is also offered. Send a SASE plus one loose stamp to: Videx, Box 1664, Stow, Ohio 44224

✦ The Direct Mail Order Association. Many services, benefits ad discounts are available to you when you join this association for a small annual fee. Commissions can also be earned when you sign up a new member. Send a SASE plus one loose stamp to: Videx, Box 1664, Stow, Ohio 44224

✦ Subscribe to Mail Order Dynamite. An excellent mail order publication dealership that pays you like an MLM company for 4 levels. Save on advertising while you earn profits recruiting new subscribers. For details send SASE plus one loose stamp to: Videx, Box 1664, Stow, Ohio 44224

✦ Earn up to 100% commission mailing circulars. This program,Big Money Can Make you Happy, offers six circular mailing offers with huge commissions. There is nothing to stock or ship—just forward the orders for shipping. Send a SASE plus one loose stamp to: Videx, Box 1664, Stow, Ohio 44224

✦ Strike it Rich with the "Franklin Income Program." Become an authorized dealer. You receive circulars for mail order programs and have your orders drop-shipped for you. There is no product to stock or ship. Send a SASE plus one loose stamp to: Videx Box 1664, Stow, Ohio 44224

✦ A stamp generating dealership. Cash . . . stamps . . . FREE Kodak film! With this offer, receive a camera ready copy and reprint rights to the circular. A coupon book for Kodak film, first class postage stamps and commission will be yours. Send a SASE plus one loose stamp to: Videx, Box 1664, Stow, Ohio 44224

✦ American Mail Marketing Opportunities Magazine. Earn $50.00 FREE advertising. When you subscribe to this magazine you will receive $50.00 worth of free advertising as well as authorization to promote the magazine allowing you to earn commission on every subscription you sell. Send a SASE plus one loose stamp to: Videx, Box 1664, Stow, Ohio 44224

✦ The Gumball Express. A large tabloid mail order publication wants your advertising business and will help you earn money while advertising your business opportunity. Receive a full one year subscription plus advertising discounts! Plus, you may become a dealer AND a distributor and earn large profits! For details, send a SASE plus one loose stamp to: Videx, Box 1664, Stow, Ohio 44224

✦ Get top quality advertising plus cash with "Ben Frank's" Almanac Dealership. This fine color tabloid offers a dealership and distributorship with typesetting and advertising opportunities. Send SASE plus one loose stamp to: Videx, Box 1664, Stow, Ohio 44224

✦ "Things I Wish Mother Had Told Me (before I got started in mail order)" If you act right now, you will get a Dealer's Profit Pack and authorization to sell this book and how to earn $10.00 commissions! Send SASE and one loose stamp to: Videx, Box 1664, Stow, Ohio 44224

✦ Mail King Plan. Get free mailing lists, stamps and money. Earn money, stamps and cash by promoting this dealership package. Send a SASE plus one loose stamp to: Videx Box 1664, Stow, Ohio 44224

✦ Mail-Courier Express. When you subscribe to Mail-Courier Express some of the benefits you receive are 6 issues of the magazine, discount on advertising, a discount on typesetting and much more including a dealership offer. Send a SASE plus one loose stamp to: Videx, Box 1664, Stow, Ohio 44224

✦ Entrepreneur's SUPER JACKPOT! This dealership will pay you weekly for promoting Entrepreneur Digest. Low cost, only $20.00! Send SASE for details to: Videx, Box 1664, Stow, Ohio 44224

✦ Illustrated Adsheet Directory. This offer is for publishers of adsheets, tabloids, etc. A dealership plan is included. Send a SASE plus one loose stamp to: Videx, Box 1664, Stow, Ohio 44224

✦ M.O.R.E. Directory. (Mail Order Related Entrepreneurs Directory) Get your name listed in this directory for a full year and you can advertise and sell this directory. For details, send SASE and one loose stamp to: Shooting Star Publications, P.O. Box 51007, Indian Orchard, MA 01151

✦ Wealth Information Network (WIN). Join the WIN program and receive six mail order benefits including dealership for this program. Send SASE plus one loose stamp for circular and details to: Jobs, P.O. Box 12417, Las Vegas, NV 89112

✦ Thinking of publishing an adsheet? Adsheet design service and dealership. For details, send SASE plus one loose stamp to: George Norr, P.O. Box 70268, Salt Lake City, UT 84170

✦ Income opportunity seekers mailing lists. Current mail order name lists with a guaranteed cash refund for undeliverable names. Three sets of aged names are available (guarantee changes with the age of the names.) These names are of people who have expressed interest in an income opportunity offer. Send SASE plus one loose stamp to: Perfect Mailing List Co., P.O. Box 1974, Memphis, TN 38101

✦ The Work-At-Home Sources Directory. Now you can find profitable work at home. New directory lists many types of home operated businesses available today. Many illustrations. There also is a dealership program with this offer. Send a SASE plus one loose stamp to: Steven Milot, 241 Main St., Fern Glen, PA 18241

✦ Home mailers needed immediately. This company states, "We pay up To $978.00 per week! Your part is simple. You simply stuff envelopes, seal them, and apply address labels and postage stamps." For details, send a SASE plus one loose stamp to: Wilson Stone, 24843 Del Prado, Suite 324, Dana Point, CA 92629

✦ Join this printing club and get a 20% discount on your printing, and earn a $10.00 credit coupon for each new member that you recruit. For complete details, send a SASE plus one loose stamp to: Chuck Rollason, 63 Main St., Dallaston, PA 17313

✦ Keep $6.00 on every $8.00 order! Get a copy of the publication, "How To Parlay Any Multi-Level Program Into a Million or More!" Send $8.00 for your copy, or send SASE for circular to: Dale Advertising, Inc., P.O. Drawer 279, Grover, NC 28073

✦ Jetstream Express. Earn $25.00 cash commission for each and every copy you sell of our special report, "How To Win In Today's MLM." For details, send SASE and one loose stamp to: Jetstream Express, 8417 Oswego Road, Suite 182, Baldwinville, NY 13027

✦ The Classified Connection. Multi-level marketing's most profitable, most professional monthly publication! How to earn $600.00 cash commission with only 3 subscribers! Send a SASE plus one loose stamp to: Catallina Publishing Corp., P.O. Box 4595, Ithaca, NY 14852

✦ Free advertising for life. This program will print your ad at very reasonable prices in a quality publication for opportunity seekers with a circulation of 5,000. When you place your ad you are automatically given an ID number to promote the plan and earn free advertising. Send a SASE and one loose stamp to: GAP Services, P.O. Box 79428 N. Dartmouth, MA 02747

✦ Gwen's Consolidated Mail. 80% commission dealership opportunity. Low advertising rates plus commission. Send a SASE and one loose stamp to: Gwen Franklin 3316 Kingsbridge Drive, Plano, TX 75075

✦ World Business Ad Club. When you purchase a lifetime membership you also receive a free display and a free classified ad, 20% discount on your ads, a commission on ads you sell and place for others. Send a SASE and one loose stamp to: Globeco Publishing Co., 1408 Baylis St., Duluth, MN 55811

✦ How To Write Headlines That Pull. Dealers wanted! Keep all the money on the 8 page booklet. Send a SASE and one loose stamp to: William H. Fordham, 146-15 133rd Ave., Jamaica, NY 11436

✦ Memberships available. Send SASE plus one loose stamp to: C.R. Johnson, 3322 Kelox Road, Baltimore, MD 21207

✦ Let's Make Some Money program. Home operated business offer with company backing including an easy to read manual. Send a SASE and one loose stamp to: David Dye, Box 1002, Battle Creek, MI 49016

✦ Daily cash mailing program. Several circular offers are included in this program where you mail the circulars for cash. Send a SASE and one loose stamp to: Independent Business Systems, P.O. Box 597, Kenansville, NC 28349

✦ Success Today. This program provides you with all the things you need to start a mail order business. Some of the things included are commissions for every sale, postage stamp commissions as well as dollar commissions, your ad printed and mailed to over 2,500. Send a SASE and one loose stamp to: F.S.T., P.O. Box 1188, Fremont, OH 43420

✦ 150 Firms That Pay You To Work At Home. This company has selected the 150 best companies to work at home for enabling you to make extra or full income. Send a SASE plus one loose stamp to: Fun Mates Press, P.O. Box 426466, San Francisco, CA 94142

✦ Once A Month Association. Now, you can have an excellent source of income with dynamic growth potential. You receive $10 for everyone that you sponsor! For details, send a SASE plus one loose stamp to: Steve Milot, 241 Main Street, Fern Glen, PA 18241

✦ Sell mailing lists. These mailing lists are current mail order and MLM prospects. A dealership offer is included. Send a SASE plus one loose stamp to: TNT Books, P.O. Box 681519, Miami, FL 33168

✦ InterNAPMOD. Earn commissions for every new member you get plus you get a commission on their renewal and more when you become a registered member. Send a SASE plus one loose stamp to: InterNAPMOD, 12 Westerville Square, Westerville, OH 43081

✦ Mail Order Mania Club. Sell commission circulars. Everything is handled for you by M.O.M. Newsletter is published periodically. Send a SASE plus one loose stamp to: M.O.M. Club P.O. Box 1188, Fremont, OH 43420

✦ Earn $500 per page with your adsheet. 100% commission dealership. Dealerships now available. For more details, send SASE and one loose stamp to: Adman, 6460-65 Convoy Court, San Diego, CA 92117-2312

✦ Join the Mail-order IBM Compatible Computer User Group. You receive 8 benefits including an exclusive commission dealership earning $10.00 for each new member that you recruit. For details send SASE plus one loose stamp to: Topscore Software, 80 Seward #C-2, Detroit, MI 48202

✦ Dealership for opportunity mailing lists. Earn 50% commission for quality mailing lists! This company can supply 5,000 fresh names per month. For details send SASE plus one loose stamp to: Paul Wilson, P.O. Box 26418, Tamarac, FL 33320

✦ Hop Aboard the Money Express! This unique program is selling a book titled, "101 Money Making Secrets" and you get paid four levels deep although this is not a MLM program. For more details, send SASE plus one loose stamp to: Fast Start Team, Box 70268, Salt Lake City, UT 84170

✦ Big Mails = Big Money! Get paid $9.95 for each big mail you send! Dealerships benefits for you to earn 100% on each new dealer that you recruit. For details, send SASE plus one loose stamp to: Beverly A. Smith, 537 W. Hopocan Avenue, Barberton, OH 44203

✦ "NO FAIL" Stamp Program. Get thousands of first-class stamps FREE! Send SASE and one loose stamp for circular and details. Networking Exchange, P.O. Box 205, Columbus, OH 43216-2905

✦ Join North American Book Dealers Exchange. If you would like to sell or publish books, this company has a unique program. Here are some of the benefits you receive as a NABE member:

- A two year subscription to "Book Dealers World," a magazine for publishers and mail order book sellers.

- FREE copy of the Book Dealer's Dropship Directory, plus dropship and wholesale dealer information.

- Several advertising savings and discounts in the Book Dealers World magazine.

- Recruit other members to join NABE and keep 50% profit for yourself.

For more information, send a SASE plus one loose stamp to: North American Bookdealers Exchange, P.O. Box 606 Cottage Grove, OR 97424

✦ Receive four of the best 50% commission, camera ready 8 1/2" x 11" dealerships in mail-order. Send $5.00 plus three loose stamps to: Thad Gajda, Box, 46247 Bedford, OH 44146

✦ Avon Products, 9 W. 57th St., New York, NY 10019 — Beauty and personal care products

✦ A. P. Programs, Inc., P.O. Box 88030, Seattle, WA 98188

✦ Act II Jewelry, Inc., Leyland Court, Bensenville, IL 60106

✦ Afton Jojoba, Inc., P.O. Box 156, Gilbert, AZ 85234 — Jojoba Products Aloe Magic

✦ AID Systems, 2674 E. Main St. #C, Ventura, CA 93003 — Record Keeping

✦ Aloe Vera Products, Inc., P.O. Box 28211, Tempe, AZ 85282 — Aloe Vera products

✦ Aloha Spirit Club, 1750 Kalakaua Ave. #3140, Honolulu, HI 96826

✦ American Bionics, Inc., 8135 Cox's Dr., Kalamazoo, MI — Aloe Vera & cleaning products

✦ American Free Enterprise, P.O. Box 1013, Sedalia, MO 65301

✦ American Professional Marketing, P.O. Box 19140, Oklahoma City, OK 73114

✦ Amsoil, Inc., Amsoil Building, Superior, WI 54880

✦ Arizona Aloe Vera Co., P.O. Box 579, Mesa, AZ 85201 — Aloe Vera Products

✦ Artistic Impressions, 240 Cortland Ave., Lombard, IL 60148 — Decorative art

✦ Amway Corp., 7575 Fulton St. East, Ada, MI 49355 — Cosmetics and skin care products

✦ Beeline Fashions, 100 Beeline Dr., Bensenville, IL 60100

✦ Better Living Aloe Vera, 5120 Hampton Ct., Wis Rapids, WI 54494 — Aloe Vera

✦ Better Living Products, 495 A Busse Road, Elk Grove Village, IL 60007

✦ Bio Line, Inc., 9201 Penn Ave. S. #10, Minneapolis, MN 55431 — Health

✦ Burgess Health Products, 7240 SE 71st Ave., Portland, OR 98206 — Health

✦ Bus Opp. Mailings, P.O. Box 8068, Fountain Valley, CA 92703

✦ C.W. Concepts, Inc., P.O. Box 1464, San Jose, CA 95109 — Computer records

✦ Cambridge Plan Int'l., Garden Road, Monterey, CA 93940 — Diet products

✦ CAPS, Inc., P.O. Box V, Castle Rock, CO 80104 — Business information management

✦ CARCO, P.O. Box 528, Belleville, IL 62222

✦ Carefree, Int'l., 1725 Hurd Drive, Irving, TX 75062 — Cosmetic & nutrition

✦ Cher Bell Creations, P.O. Box 341028, Memphis, TN 38134 — Aloe Vera

✦ Chrissie Cosmetics, Inc., 6124 Harne Ave., Shreveport, LA 71108 — Cosmetics

✦ Collegedale Diversified Enterprises, P.O. Box 1143, Collegedale, TN 37315

✦ Communication Network, Inc., 3605 Quentin Road, Brooklyn, NY 11234

✦ Crabtree Mint, 6022 Skyway, Paradise, CA 95969

✦ D.W. Ford Corp., 1620 Centinela Ave. #202, Inglewood, CA 90302

✦ DecoPlantMinder, 22582 Shannon Circle, Lake Forest, CA 92630

✦ Discovery Toys, 2530 Arnold Dr. #400, Martinez, CA 94553 — Games and toys

✦ Discovery World Int'l., P.O. Box 52, North Salt Lake City, UT 84054

✦ Diversified Unlimited, Inc., 215 W. Main, Cabot, AR 72023

✦ Don M Company, 1215 S. Bennett, Tyler, TX 75701 — Aloe Vera products

✦ Dyna LIFE, Inc., 2160 Bradford St., Clearwater, FL 33520

✦ Envrio Tech International, 6600 W Charleston #125, Las Vegas, NV 89102 — Free car wash/protective sealant

✦ Executive Marketing, P.O. Box 65, Clayton, NJ 08312

✦ Financial Success Institute, P.O. Box 1106, Cary, NC 2 7512 — Personal financial/improvement products and services

✦ First Fitness Int'l. Inc., 15944 Midway Rd., Dallas, TX 75244 — Beauty and health related products

✦ First Rate Enterprises, 413 Elmwood, Troy, MI 48084

✦ For You, Inc., P.O. Box 1216, Loris, SC 29669 — Personal care products

✦ Forever Living Products, P.O. Box 29041, Phoenix, AZ 85038 — Aloe Vera products

✦ Fortunate Corp., Box 5604, Charlottesville, VA 22905 — Health & beauty

✦ Franklin Marketing, P.O. Box 40291, Cincinnati, OH 45240 — Soap & Shampoos

✦ Free Enterprise Alliance, P.O. Box 828, San Diego, CA 92015

✦ Gameworld, 1314 LaLoma, Berkeley, CA 94708

✦ Genesis Plant Products, 709 N. Nevada #207, Colorado Springs, CO 80903

✦ Geographics, Inc., P.O. Box R1, Blaine, WA 98230

✦ Golden Dawn, P.O. Box 2231, Garland, TX 75041 — Aloe Vera products

✦ Golden Pride, 1501 Northpoint Pkwy. #100, West Palm Beach, FL 33407 — Health care/nutritional supplements/pet

✦ Golden Wunder, P.O. Box C4320, Scottsdale, AZ 858261

✦ Helen Marie, Inc., P.O. Box 1000, Derry, NH 03038

✦ Herbalife, P.O. Box 80210, Los Angeles, CA 90301 — Health related/skin and hair products

✦ Herbalife Int'l., 5741 Buckingham Hts. Pkwy., Culver City, CA 90230

✦ Health, Home Galleries, Leyland Court, Bensenville, IL 60106

✦ House of Lloyd, Inc., 11901 Grandview Rd., Grandview, MO 64030 — Kitchen related products, gifts

✦ Hurley Chicago Co., 7011 S. 11th St., Worth, IL 60482 — Water filters

✦ Image Dynamics, 2511 S.W. Temple, Salt Lake City, UT 84115

✦ Int'l. Home Shopping, AmerHome ShopPlaza, Canton, OH 44767

✦ Jay Clark Co., 5328 Central Ave., St. Petersburg, FL 33707 — Business Products

✦ Jerical Financial, 6872 Georgetown Circle, Anaheim, CA 92807

✦ Jeunique International, Inc., 19501 E Walnut Dr., City Of Industry, CA 91749 — Cosmetics/nutritional products/lingerie

✦ JMark Services, 167 N. 400 West, Salt Lake City, UT 84103

✦ Kal-Son House, 600 Shepard Tower, Minneapolis, MN 55426

✦ La Societe "Savoir Faire" Int'l., 90 S. Wadsworth Blvd., #105, Denver, CO 80226

✦ L'Arome, 456 Lakeshore Pkwy, Rockhill, SC 29730 — Health care related products/fragrances

✦ Life Products, P.O. Box 0445, San Clemente, CA 92672 — Sports & fitness

✦ Life Time Management, 175 S. Fair Oaks, Pasadena, CA 91105 — Time management

✦ Light Force, 1115 Thompson Ave. #5, Santa Cruz, CA 95062 — Nutritional products

✦ Mannaya, Inc., 200 Executive Dr., Brookfield, WI 53005 — Health products

✦ Marketing, 5328 Central Ave., St. Petersburg, FL 33707

✦ Mary Kay Cosmetics, 8787 Stemmons Freeway., Dallas, TX 75247 — Cosmetics and skin care products

✦ McNess Co., 120 E. Clark St., Freeport, IL 61032,

✦ Meadow Fresh Farms, Inc., P.O. Box 30105, Salt Lake City, UT 84130

✦ Melaleuca Inc., 3910 S Yellowstone, Idaho Falls, ID 83402 — Nutritional/personal and home care products

✦ Money Tree Express, P.O. Box 2456, White City, OR 97503

✦ Multi-Level Sales Assn., 601 S. Venice Blvd. #4335, Venice, CA 90291

✦ National Diamond Exchange, 400 Tidd Drive, Galion, OH 44833

✦ Natural World, Inc., 652 Glenbrook Rd., Stamford, CT 07906 — Household/personal products environment friendly

✦ Nature's Choice, 3101 N. Federal Hwy., Ste. 506, Fort Lauderdale, FL 33306

✦ Nature's Sunshine Products, 75 E 1700, South Provo, UT 94605 — Herbs, vitamins and personal care products

✦ Nema, Inc., P.O. Box 7003, Muncie, IN 47305

✦ Neo Life, Co., 25000 Industrial Blue, Hayward, CA 94545

✦ Nest Egg Society, P.O. Box 100129, Ft. Lauderdale, FL 33310

✦ Network Marketing Group, 8885 SW Canton Road, Portland, OR 97225

✦ New Generation, P.O. Box 20160, Reno, NV 89515 — Shampoo & hair conditioners

✦ N-Joy Products, Inc., 3125 52nd Ave., Sacramento, CA 95823

✦ Noevir Inc, 1095 SE Main St., Irvine CA 92714 — Personal care products

✦ NonPerre, 4879 E La Palma Ave. #206, Anaheim Hills, CA 92807 — skin/body/hair care products

✦ NuSkin International, 1 Provo Ctr., Provo, UT 84606 — Cosmetics & health care products

✦ Olde World, Inc., P.O. Box 2488, High Point, NC 27261

✦ Omnitrition, 1620 Rafe St. #108, Carollton, TX 75006 — Nutritional products

✦ Oriflame Corp., 76 Treble Cove Rd., No Billerica, MA 01862

✦ Cosmetics, P. I. Distributors, P.O. Box 1400, Shingle Springs, CA 95682

✦ Personal Wealth Systems, 8535 25 Bay Meadows Rd., Jacksonville, FL — Financial & personal development

✦ Preferred Mktg Assn., 9019 Park Plaza Dr. #H, La Mesa, CA 92041

✦ Print Shoppe, Inc., 1915 Southeastern Ave., Indianapolis, IN 46201

✦ Priority Products, 2300 SE Belmont St., Portland, OR 98214 — Nutritional Products

✦ R & L Club, 9406 Bataan St, Minneapolis, MN 55434

✦ Regal Ware, Inc., 1675 Reigle Dr, Kewaskum, WI 53040

✦ Rexair, 3221 W. Big Beaver Rd. #200, Troy, MI 48084 — Vacuum cleaners

✦ Rexall Sundown International, Broken Sound Parkway, Boca Raton, FL 33309 — Nutritional products

✦ Robert Charles Assoc, P.O. Box 911, Lake Mary, FL 3274

✦ Royal American Food Co, P.O. Box 1000, Blue Springs, MO 64015

✦ Sales Game, Inc., P.O. Box 17405, Salt Lake City, UT 84117

✦ Sarah Coventry, Inc., Sarah Coventry Pkwy, Newark, NJ 14593

✦ SASCO, 2300 Valley View Ln. #230, Farmers Branch, TX 75234 — Skin and health related products

✦ Sasco Cosmetics, 2151 Hutton Dr., Carrollton, TX 75006 — Personal Care

✦ Shaklee Corp., 444 Market St., San Francisco, CA 94111 — Skin care/food/cleaning/nutritional products

✦ Southeast Marketing, 12374 Aladdin Road, Jacksonville, FL 32223

✦ Star Plus, 232 W. 90th South, Sandy, UT 84070

✦ Sun Marketing Group, P.O. Box 25130, Tamarac, FL — Vitamins & diet program

✦ Sunasu Int'l., P.O. Box 82144, San Diego, CA 92138 — Nutritional products

✦ Sunrider Corp., P.O. Box 2020, Provo, UT 84603 — Chinese Herbal Concentrate

✦ Super Nutrition, 531 44th Ave., San Francisco, CA 94121 — Nutritional

✦ Taylor Care Co., 2008 Fuller Road, Des Moines, IA 50265

✦ Fuller Brush Co., The, 3065 Center Green Dr., Boulder, CO 80301 — Household cleaning products

✦ The NANCI Corp., 7633 E. 63rd Pl., Tulsa, OK 74133 — Nutritional supplements

✦ Total Success, Inc., P.O. Box 5540, Scottsdale, AZ 85261 — Health related

Directory of mail order services and suppliers

14

Chapter 14

Directory of mail order services and suppliers

This directory contains a listing of companies that offer their services and products by mail. Most of these companies have been in business for a number of years and have an excellent reputation. You will probably find the service and products that you can purchase from these companies are often better and more competitive than your local sources. This directory is categorized for your convenience.

Professional writing & publishing organizations

American Bookdealers Exchange—Box 606, Cottage Grove, OR 97424

American Bookseller Association—1222 42nd St., New York, NY 10168

American Library Association—50 E Huron St., Chicago, IL 60611

Authors Guild—234 W. 44th St., New York, NY 10036

Book Publicists of Southern California—6430 Sunset Blvd., #503,

Hollywood, CA 90028

Cosmep—P.O. Box 703, San Francisco, CA 94101

Direct Marketers Association—6 East 43rd Street, New York, NY 10017

Independent Publishers Network—P.O. Box 546, El Cajon, CA 92022

Marin Self-Publishers Association—P.O. Box 343, Ross, CA 94957

Money Club—5818 N. 7th Street #103, Phoenix, AZ 85014

National Mail Order Association—5818 Venice Blvd., Los Angeles, CA 90019

National Writers Club—1450 S. Havana #620, Aurora, CO 80012

Publishers Marketing Association—P.O. Box 299, Hermosa Beach, CA 90254

Mail order book publishers

These are the major mail-order type book distributors and publishers who offer a wide selection. Write and request information on available dealerships and catalogs.

American Bookdealers Exchange—Box 606, Cottage Grove, OR 97424

ARCO Publishing Co.—215 Park Ave. S, New York, NY 10003

Book World Promotions, Inc.—87-93 Christie St., Newark, NJ 07105

Cuppett Enterprises—P.O. Box 91, Wilmington, CA 90748

Jeffrey Lant Associates—50 Follen St. Ste. 507, Cambridge, MA 02138

M.O.R.E.—305 E Main St. Goessel, KS 67053

Mascor Publishing Co.—P.O. Box 8308, Silver Spring, MD 20907

Mitchell Enterprises—204 Oakdale, Pasadena, TX 77506

Outlet Book Co.—225 Park Ave. S, New York, NY 10016

Overstock Book Co.—120 Secatogue Ave, Farmingdale, NY 11735

Premier Publishers, Inc.—Box 330309, Ft. Worth, TX 76163

Profit Ideas—254 E. Grand Ave., Escondido, CA 92025

Publishers Marketing Ent.— 386 Park Ave. S, New York, NY 10016

S & L Sales—P.O. Box 2067 Waycross, GA 31501

Selective Books, Inc.—P.O. Box 1140, Clearwater, FL 33517

Stew Caverly—216 McLean St., Wilkes-Barre, PA 18702

Western Book Distributors—2970 San Pablo Ave., Berkeley, CA 94702

Wilshire Book Co.—12015 Sherman Road, North Hollywood, CA 91605

Major book publishers

You may want to get on the mailing list of these publishers. Many times they offer bargain closeouts!

Addison-Wesley Pub. Co.—Jacob Way, Reading, MA 01867

Charles Scribner & Sons—866 3rd Ave., New York, NY 10022

Dell Publishing Co., Inc.—1 Dag Hammarskj Old Plaza, New York, NY 10017

Doubleday & Co., Inc.—245 Park Ave., New York, NY 10167

Farnsworth Publishing Co.—78 Randall Ave., Rockville Centre, NY 11570

Fleming Revell Co.—Central Ave., Old Tappan, NJ 07675

Harper & Rowe Books—10 E 53rd St., New York, NY 10022

Little, Brown & Co.—34 Beacon St., Boston, MA 02108

Lyle Stuart, Inc.—120 Enterprise Ave., Secaucus, NJ 07094

McGraw-Hill Book Co.—1221 Ave. of the Americas, New York, NY 10020

Nelson-Hall Publishers—111 N. Canal St., Chicago, IL 60606

Prentice-Hall, Inc.—Business Book Division Englewood, NJ 07632

Random House, Inc.—201 E. 50th St., New York, NY 10022

Simon & Schuster—1230 Ave. of the Americas, New York, NY 10020

St. Martin's Press—175 5th Ave., New York, NY 10010

W.W. Norton Co., Inc.—500 5th Ave., New York, NY 10110

William Morrow & Co.—105 Madison Ave., New York, NY

Graphic art supplies & services

Clip Art

A. H. Gaebel, Inc.—P.O. Box 5 E., Syracuse, NY 13057

Art Master—500 N. Claremont Blvd., Claremont, CA 91711

Bob Constable—Box 354, Christmas, FL 32709

Creative Media—P.O. Box 5955, Berkeley, CA 94705

Dynamic Graphics—6000 N. Forest Park Dr., Peoria, IL 61656

Graphics Master—P.O. Box 46086, Los Angeles, CA 90046

Free-Lance Graphic Artists

Adman—6460-65 Convoy Court, San Diego, CA 92117

Beysso Enterprise—2215A Scovel Ave., Pennsauken, NJ 08110

Gray Studios—P.O. Box 811, Levittown, PA 19058

LOGO Designers—948 Willow Court, Hammond, IN 46320

William H. Fordham—146-15 133rd Ave., Jamaica, NY 11436

Graphic art supplies

Dot Pasteup Supplies—1612 California St., Omaha, NE 68102

Graphic Products Corp.— 3601 Edison Place, Rolling Meadows, IL 60008

Hartco Products—West Jefferson, OH 43162

Midwest Publishers Supply—4640 N. Olcott Ave., Chicago, IL 60656

National Laser Separations, Inc.—3501 NW 67th St., Miami, FL 33147

Toucan Scan—407 NW 16th Ave., Portland, OR 97209

Typesetting

Ashley Advertising, Inc.—P.O. Box 20822 , Portland, OR 97220

CHS Enterprises—P.O. Box 160 Uncasville, CT 06382

JAMART Services—13127 Tilden Avenue, Champlin, MN 55316

Pete Skeberdis—Box 27 Fremont, MI 49312

Wolf Enterprises—104 Cassidy Ct., Cary, NC 27511

Typing services

Mailathon, Inc.—16 Van Wetering Pl, Hackensack, NJ 07601

Steve Lockman—P.O. Box 137, Lancaster, MN 56735

Magazines

These are some of the best of well-known mail-order publications. Write and request a sample copy of their publication. If you make it known that you are interested in placing advertising, they will generally send you a free sample with advertising rates.

Alps Monthly—P.O. Box 99394, San Francisco, CA 94109

Artcraft Press—P.O. Box 225 Mankato, MN 56001

Ben Frank's Almanac—P.O. Box 655, Pinellas Park, FL 34664

Book Dealers World—P.O. Box 606, Cottage Grove, OR 97424

Cosmep Newsletter—P.O. Box 703 San Francisco, CA 94101

Direct Response Specialist—P.O. Box 1075, Tarpon Springs, FL 34286

Direct Response Profit Report—P.O. Box 546, El Cajon, CA 92022

Direct Marketing Magazine—224 Seventh St., Garden City, NY 11530

DM News—19 W. 21st St., New York, NY 10010

Emerald Coast News—P.O. Box 190, Niceville, FL 32578

Entrepreneur's Digest—P.O., Box 3224 Oshkosh, WI 54904

Golden Opportunities—P.O. Box 690, Hallsville, TX 75650

Hi-Lite Harris House—P.O. Box 101, DeSota, MO 63020

Idea Digest—P.O. Box 80, Foyil, OK 74031

Income & Small Business Opportunities—2002 London Road #101,

Duluth, MN 55812

Income Opportunities—380 Lexington Ave., New York, NY 10017

Lee Howard Newsletter—P.O. Box 1140, Clearwater, FL 34617

Mail Order Messenger—P.O. Box 17131, Memphis, TN 38187

Mail Order Dynamite—P.O. Box 681519, Miami, FL 33168

Mail Profits Magazine—P.O. Box 4785 Lincoln, NE 68504

Mail Courier Express—P.O. Box 1505, Richmond, CA 94802

Money Making Opportunities—11071 Ventura Blvd., Studio City, CA 100117

Opportunity Connection Magazine—P.O. Box 57723, Webster, TX 77598

Opportunity Magazine—73 Spring St., New York, NY 10012

Profit Gems Marketing—P.O. Box 3087, Jekyll Island, GA 31520

RMH Opportunities—4615 Takilma Road, Cave Junction, OR 97523

Sabal House—P.O. Box 937, DeBary, FL 32713

Salesman's Opportunity Magazine—Suite 405, 6 N. Michigan Ave.,

Chicago, IL 60602

Small Press Review—P.O. Box 100, Paradise, CA 95969

Spare Time Magazine—5810 W. Oklahoma Ave., Milwaukee, WI 53219

Spare Time Money-Making Opportunities—5810 W. Okla. Ave., Milwaukee, WI 53219 Specialty Salesman Magazine—6285 Barfield Road, Atlanta, GA 30328

The Huenefeld Report—P.O. Box U, Bedford, MA 01730

Towers Club Newsletter—P.O. Box 2038, Vancouver, WA 98668

Mail-order & MLM promotional services

Classified advertising agencies

National Classified Network—4343 N.W. Highway, Dallas, TX 75220

National Mailorder Classified—Box 5, Sarasota, FL 34230

Mailing list brokers

Accredited Mailing Lists, Inc.—5272 River Rd.,Washington, DC 20016

Action Markets—1710 Highway 35, Ocean, NJ 07712

Advon—P.O. Drawer 1, Shelly, ID 83274

AIM Lists—P.O. Box 22822, San Diego, CA 92192

Alvin B. Seller—475 Park Ave. South, New York, NY 10016

Best Lists—P.O. Box 56, Lakeville, OH 44638

Bocca Direct—472 36th St., Manhattan Beach, CA 90266

C.B. Graphics—339 Mid Country Rd., Selden, NY 11784

Current List Productions—776 E. Edison, Manteca, CA 95236

Datatech Communications—351 Pike Blvd., #130-106 Lawrenceville, GA 30245

DAX Mail Lists—Box 14 Williamston, MI 48895

Dunhill Int'l—630 Third Ave., New York, NY 10017

Ed Burnett—99 W. Sheffield Ave., Englewood, NJ 07631

Enterprise Lists—725 Market St., Wilmington, DE 19801

Group One Communications—P.O. Box 1560, Jensen Beach, FL 34958

Hank Marshall—P.O. Box 2729, Laguna Hills, CA 92653

Harris House—P.O. Box 101, DeSota, MO 63020

Hugo Dunhill Mailing Lists—630 Third Ave. New York, NY 10017

Imperial Mail Lists—4005 Manzanita Ave., Suite 6-228, Carmichael,CA 95608

Jaydee Lists—P.O. Box 16, Stanford, CT 06497

Kelly Company—639 Shadow Creek Drive, San Jose, CA 5136

Lelli Printing—2650 CR 175, Loudonville, OH 44842

List World—555 Sparkman, Huntsville, AL 35816

List Masters—P.O. Box 750, Wantagh, NY 11793

LPM Associates—Box 133, Elmont, NY 11003

Luxury Life Network—P.O. Box 17080, Plantation, FL 33318

McAfee & Co.—1815 Carpenter St.,Bridgeport, TX 76026

National Mail Lists—411 Deese Road, Ozark, AL 36360

National Promotions—P.O. Box 1547, Bloomfield, NJ 07003

P. Wagoner—10250 April Rd. Salineville, OH 43945

Perfict Mail Lists—P.O. Box 174, Memphis, TN 38101

Premier Publishers—P.O. Box 330309, Ft. Worth, TX 76163

Quality Mail Lists—P.O. Box 1305, Seaford, NY 11783

Quality Mail Lists—P.O. Box 6060, Miller Place, NY 11764

Real Value Enterprises—P.O. Box 372 Franklin, PA 16323

Redford Publications—P.O. Box 967, Willingboro, NJ 08064

S.E. Ring—Box 372, Fort Lauderdale, FL 33318

Selmar-Brooks Pub.—126 Homecrest Station, Brooklyn, NY 11229

Trade Winds Marketing—31 Tracy Rd, New Paltz, NY 12561

Unicorn—P.O. Box 231 Decatur, IL 62525

Venture—P.O. Box 336, Riviera, AZ 86442

Watermamte Marketing Co.—13735 Bl # 1, Van Nuys, CA 91401

Postcard pack mailers

Jeffery Lant—50 Follen St. Suite 507, Cambridge, MA 02138

Select Info Exchange—244 West 54th, 7th FL, New York, NY 10012

The Trump Card Marketing—1340 Teaneck Road, Teaneck, NJ 07666

The Media Organization, Inc.—Box 49, Syosset, NY 11791

Venture Communications—60 Madison Avenue, New York, NY 10010

Visual Horizons—180 Metro Park, Rochester, NY 14623

Print & mail services

Bookworm Benny Inc.—P.O. Box 1007, New Hyde Park, NY 11040

Carl T. O'Shea—P.O. Box 700, Baldin Park, CA 91706

G & B Records—P.O. Box 10150, Terra Bella, CA 93270

JRS Printing & Advertising—P.O. Box 2580, Calcutta, OH 43920

Larry Chiappone—936 11th St. Box 1125, West Babylon, NY 11704

Lelli Printing & Advertising—2650 CR 175, Loudonville, OH 4842

Sabal House—P.O. Box 937, DeBary, FL 32713

Watts Wholesale Co.—7824 Whites Creek Pk., Joelton, TN 37080

Office supplies & services

Computer Services

Adoniram—P.O. Box 786 Ft. Worth, TX 76101

AFC Computed Services—370 Seventh Ave., New York, NY 11530

Anchor Computer—750 Zeckendorf Blvd., Garden City, NY 11530

CCX—301 Industrial Blvd., Conway, AR 72032

Creative Mailings, Inc.—20850 Leapwood, Carson, CA 90746

Data Services—49 Valley, Furlong, Pa 18925

DM Data Services— 814 Eagle Dr., Bensenville, IL 60106

Enertex Computer Concepts—444 Park Ave.S, New York, NY 10016

Hallmark Data Systems, Inc.—5500 Touhy Ave., Skokie, IL 60106

Mailing Data Services, Inc.—510 E. Commercial St., Los Angeles, CA 90021

MS Data Service Corp.—10221 Slater Ave. #112, Fountain Valley, CA 92708

New Processing Corp.—7650 E. Redfield Rd. Ste. 2, Scottsdale, AZ 85260

Printronic Corp.—10 Columbus Circle, New York, NY 10019

Speedata Ltd—1200 Shames Dr., Westbury, NY 11590

Computer supplies

Devoke Data Products—1500 Martin Ave., Santa Clara, CA 95050

Executive Computer Supplies—P.O. Box 5153, Largo, FL 33540

Mail Advertising Supply Co.—P.O. Box 363, Waukesha, WI 53187

MISCO—One Misco Plaza, Holmdel, NJ 07733

Office supplies & products

Associates Printers, Inc.—P.O. Box 2305, E. Liverpool, OH 43920

Business Envelope Mfg.—900 Grand Blvd., Deer Park, NY 11729

Grayarc—P.O. Box 2944, Hartford, CT 06104

JEFFCO Inc.—205 Hallock Ave., Middlesex, NJ 08846

National Pen Corp.—9395 Cabot Dr., San Diego, CA 92181

NEBS—500 Main St., Groton, MA 01470

Nordisco Corporation—5703 W. Howard St., Niles, IL 60618

Quill Corp.—100 S. Schelter Rd., Lincolnshire, IL 60198

Shiller & Schmidt, Inc.—3100 N. Elston Ave., Chicago, IL 60618

The Stationary House—1000 Florida Ave., Hagerstown, MD 21741

The Drawing Board—P.O. Box 220505, Dallas, TX 75222

The Business Book—One E. Eighth Ave., Oshkosh, WI 54906

The Reliable Corp.—1001 W. Van Buren St., Chicago, IL 60607

Viking Office Products—13515 S. Figueroa St., Los Angeles, CA 90061

Rubber stamps

Don Product—Box 1736, Chicago, IL 60617

Reynolds Press—432 Maple Ave., Selkirk, NY 12158

Rubber Stamp News & Supplies/Robinson Stamp Co.—

P.O. Box 415, New Hartford, NY 34133

Swedco—Box 29, Mooresville, NC 28115

Specialty book & office supplies & equipment

American Thermoplastic Co.—622 Second Ave., Pittsburgh, PA 15219

Beemak Plastics—7424 Santa Monica Blvd., Los Angles, CA 90046

Mason Box Company—512 Mt. Hope Street Box 129, North Attleboro, MA 02761

Multi-AD Services, Inc.—P.O. Box 786, Peoria, IL 61652

National Bag Co.—2233 Old Mill Rd., Hudson, OH 44236

NSC International—P.O. Box 1800, Hot Springs, AR 71902

Professional Aids—1678 S. Wolf Rd., Wheeling, IL 60090

S.L. Enterprises—443 E. Westfield Ave., Roselle Park, NJ 07204

Siegal Displays Products—P.O. Box 95, Minneapolis, MN 55440

Comstock—32 E. 31st St. New York, NY 10016

The Highsmith Co., Inc.—Highway 106 E., Ft. Atkinson, WI 53538

Vulcan Binder & Cover Co.—P.O. Box 29, Vincent, AL 35178

Special equipment

Addressograph Farrington, Inc.—Randolph Industrial Park, Randolph, MA 02368

Comtel Broadcasting Corp.—13 Harbortown Center # 61, Noblesville, IN 46060

Telemarketing Machines Equipment Brokers Unlimited—

　　3525 Old Conejo Rd. #105, Newbury Park, CA 91320

Kroy—P.O. Box 4300, Scottsdale, AZ 85261

Labels

Heins—Box 215, Port Reading, NJ 07064

Label Art, Inc.—One Riverside Way, Wilton, NH 03086

Monarch Press—P.O. Box 139, Carson City, NV 89720

Northeast Products Box 160, Haverhill, MA 01831

Promark—P.O. Box 397, Rutherford, TN 38369

Printers

Book & manual printers

Apollo Books, Inc.—107 Lafayette St., Winona, MN 55978

Book Press—Putney Rd. Brattleboro, VT 05301

Book-Mart Press, Inc.—2001 42nd St., N. Bergen, NJ 07047

Bookmasters—P.O. Box 159, Ashland, OH 44805

Braum-Brumfield, Inc.—P.O. Box 1203, Ann Arbor, MI 49503

Delta Lithograph Co.—14731 Califa St., Van Nuys, CA 91204

Eerdman's Printing Co.—231 Jefferson Ave. SE, Grand Rapids, MI 49503

Griffin Printing—544 W. Colorado St., Glendale, CO 91204

Interstate Book Mfg. 2115 E. Kansas City Rd., Olathe, KS 66061

Kingsport Press, Inc.—P.O. Box 711, Kingsport, TN 37662

KNI, Inc.—1240 S. State College Blvd., Anaheim, CA 92806

McNaughton & Gunn, Inc.—P.O. Box 2060, Ann Arbor, MI 48106

R.R. Donnelly & Sons—2223 Martin Luther King Dr., Chicago, IL 60616

Thompson-Shore, Inc.—7300 W. Joy St., Dexter, MI 48130

Business forms

Amsterdam Printing & Litho—Amsterdam, NY 12010

McBee Mail Order Forms—299 Cherry Hill Road, Parsippany, NY 07054

Moore Business Products—P.O. Box 5000, Vernon Hills, IL 60061

Pickett-Chartpak—One River Road, Leeds, MA 01053

Streamliners—P.O. Box 480, Mechanicsburg, PA 17055

Envelope manufacturers & printers

Accurate Envelope Co., Inc.—320 Lafayette St., New York, NY 10012

Artcraft Press—P.O. Box 225, Mankato, MN 56001

Business Envelope Manufacturer—900 Grand Blvd., Deer Park, NY 11729

Continental Envelope Corp.—5515 Shore Trail NE, Prior Lake, MN 55372

Design Distributors, Inc.—45 E. Industry Ct., Deer Park, NY 11729

Envelope Sales Company—Normandy, TN 37360

Envelopes Limited—899 E First St., Kansas City, MO 64106

Gilmore Envelope Co.—4540 Worth St. Los Angeles, CA 90023

Glendale Envelope Co.—634 W. Broadway, Glendale, CA 91204

Golden State Envelopes—1601 Gower St., Los Angeles, CA 90028

Gotham Envelope Corp.—1 Madison St., E. Rutherford, NJ 07073

Mil-Well Envelope Co.—809 W. Santa Anita St., San Gabriel, CA 91778

Ohio Envelope—5161 W. 164th St., Cleveland, OH 44142

Rockmont Envelope Co.—360 W. Burgatti St., Salt Lake City, UT 84115

Southwest Envelope Co.—3839 N 35th St., Phoenix, AZ 85017

Transco Envelope Co.—3542 N. Kimball Ave., Chicago, IL 60618

Triangle Envelope Co.—61 Visco Court, Nashville, TN 37210

U.S. Envelope 349 W. Tremont St., Charlotte, NC 28203

Full color printers

Brown Printing Co.—U.S. Highway 14 W, Waseca, NM 5 6093

Combo Color Co.—50 Madison St., Maywood, IL 60153

Direct Press Modern Litho—386 Oakwood Rd., Huntington Station, NY 11746

Petty Co.—41 E. 42nd St., New York, NY 10017

The Press—18780 W. 78th St., Chanhassen, MN 55317

Volkmuth Printers, Inc.—East Hwy. 23, Box 1007, St. Cloud, MN 56302

Low cost circular printers

American Mail Order Printers—300 Travis Lane, Bldg 20, Waukesha, WI 53186

Cosmos International—P.O. Box 43056, St. Louis, MO 63143

Domar Printing—308 Main St., Laurel, MD 20707

Henry Birtle Company—1143 E. Colorado St., Glendale, CA 91205

JRS Printing & Advertising—P.O. Box 2508, Calcutta, OH 43920

Lelli Printing & Advertising—2650 Cr 175 Loudonville, OH 44842

Roger Goad Printing—P.O. Box 1188, Fremont, OH 43420

USA Printing—Suite 30, 160 Washington SE, Albuquerque, NM 87108

Multi-purpose offset printers

These printers produce circulars, brochures and letterheads. They also can print booklets, reports and directories.

Big City Litho—550 N. Claremont Blvd., Claremont, CA 91711

Classic Printing Co.—7250 Auburn Bl #143, Citrus Heights, CA 95610

Creative Printing—309 S. Third St., Ironton, OH 45638

Dinner & Klein—600 S. Spokane St., Seattle, WA 98124

Dress America, Inc.—1001 Nicholas Bl., Elk Grove Village, IL 60007

Econo Printers—11565 Ridgewood Circle N, Seminole, FL 33542

Equitable Web Offset—24 New Bridge Rd., Bergenfield, NJ 07621

Fitch Graphic—P.O. Box 768500, Atlanta, GA 30328

G & G Press—P.O. Box 660813 Miami, FL 33266

Henry Birtle Co.—1143 E. Colorado St., Glendale, CA 91205

M.O.R.E. Printing—307 E. Main St., Goessel, KS 67053

Mail Order Promotions—P.O. Box 988, Lewiston, NY 14092

Mark's Printing Service—P.O. Box 308 McKeesport, PA 15134

Parkway Business Services—P.O. Box 29, Hinesville, GA 31313

Robeson Press —P.O. Box 130, Pembroke, NC 28372

Speedy Printers—23800 Aurora Rd. Bedford Hts., OH 44147

Topshelf Publications—2005 Pueblo Court, Plano, TX 75074

Two Brothers, Inc.—1602 Locust St., St. Louis, MO 63103

Web printers

Web printers specialize in long printing runs that are often produced on low-cost newsprint paper such as for tabloids, catalogs & newspapers, etc.

Des Plains Publishing Co.—1000 Executive Way, Des Plaines, IL 60018

Econo Printers—11565 Ridgewood Circle N., Seminole, FL 33542

Pomerado Publishing Co.—13247 Poway Rd., Poway, CA 92064

Sun Litho—7950 Haskell Ave., Van Nuys, CA 91406

Western Offset—348 W. Market St. #206, San Diego, CA 92101

General information

Obtaining copyright protection

To officially copyright your materials, you must write to the federal copyright office and request FORM TX with instructions. They will send to you the application form, instructions and a price list. Their address is: Copyright Office, Library of Congress, Washington, DC 20559

Free copy of government books

The U.S. Government Printing Office has a free catalog of new and popular books they sell. Subjects include agriculture, energy, children, space, health, history, business, vacations and much more. Write to: Free Catalog—P.O. Box 37000, Washington, DC 20013-7000

Wholesale Catalogs .

The following companies publish or distribute one or more wholesale, closeouts and bargain catalogs and directories. Write to them and request information and current prices.

A.B. Scotchmark International—5468 Dundas St., Suite 806,

Toronto, Ontario M9B-6E3 B.

Klein Publications—P.O. Box 8503, Coral Springs, FL 33065

Bargain Hunters—P.O. Box 1409 Holland, MI 49422

Business Network Corporation—P. O. Box 56844, Atlanta, GA 30343

Catalogs —P.O. Box 92452, Atlanta, GA 30314

Catalogue Service Center—P.O. Box 4507 Burbank, CA 91503

Consumer Marketing—P.O. Box 511, Logan, UT 84321

Damarko Company—9354 S. Dairy, Suite 1601, Ashford, TX 77099

DDN & Company—P.O. Box 20152, Ferndale, MI 48220

Dee's Wholesale Dist.—P.O. Box 1433, Greenville, NC 27835

Design News Directories—P.O. Box 188, New Town Branch, Boston, MA 02258

E.F. Lindbloom Company—3636 Peterson Ave., Chicago, IL 60659

Enterprise Magazine, Inc.—1020 Broadway, Suite 111, Milwaukee, WI 53202

Gale Research Co., Inc.—Book Tower, Dept 77748, Detroit, MI 48277

Global Business & Trade—386 East "H" St., Suite 209-255, Chula Vista, CA 92010

Grey House Publishing—Bank of Boston Building, Sharon, CT 06069

International Business Directories—P.O. Box 2167, Saipan, CT 96950

Inter'l Publications—511 Glenwood Avenue, Buffalo, NY 14208

J.S. Marketing Service—P.O. Box 7024, Greenville, NC 27835

Manufacturer's News—4 East Huron Street, Chicago, IL 60611

Marco Novelty Co.—508 South Main St.,—P.O. Box 705, Ashburn, GA 31714

McGraw Hill Information Services Company—1221 Avenue of the Americas,

New York, NY 10020

Pyramid East Publishing Co.—P.O. Box 881, Chester, VA 23831

Todd Publications—18 North Greenbush Rd., West Nyack, NY 10994

Tradeway Marketing Company—P.O. Box 411, Hopedale, MA 01747

U.S. Industrial Directory—44 Cook St., Denver, CO 80206

United Publishing Company—P.O. Box 90482, Burton, MI 48509

World Distributors—3311 W. Montrose Ave., Chicago, IL 60618

World Wide Trade Service Company—P.O. Box 283, Medina, WA 98039

Resources

••• Online Resources •••

◆ **Advertising Mail Marketing Association**
http://amma.org

◆ **American Association of Home-Based Business**
http://www.aahbb.org

◆ **American Computer Group—Mailorder.com**
http://www.mailorder.com

◆ **American Online Hometown—Mail order businesses**
http://hometown.aol.com/cat.adp?cid=21151

◆ **Direct Marketing Association**
http://www.the-dma.org

◆ **Direct Marketing Resource Center**
http://www2.womeninpackaging.orgdmcenter.html

◆ **Direct Marketing News**
   http://www.dmnews.com

◆ **Entrepreneur Magazine**
   http://www.entrepreneurmag.commarketing

◆ **4 Free Net**
   http://www.4free.net

◆ **Gale Group, The**
   http://www.thomson.comgale/default.html

◆ **Global Wealth Builders**
   http://www.gwb2000.com

◆ **Home Business Works**
   http://www.homebusinessworks.com

◆ **Listsnow.com**
   http://listsnow.com

◆ **Lycos Small Business Guide: Multi-Level Marketing**
   *http://www-srl.lycos.comwguide/wire/wire_*
   484445_47604_3_1.html

◆ **Mail Advertising Service Association International**
   http://www.masa.org

◆ **Marketing Resource Center**
   http://www.marketingsource.com

◆ **MediaFinder from Oxbridge Communications, Inc.**
   http://www.mediafinder.com

◆ **Money Maker's Monthly**
   http://www.mmmonthly.com

◆ **Multi-level Marketing Mall**
   http://www.mlm-mall.com

- **National Mail Order Association, LLC**
  http://www.nmoa.org

- **Plateau Publishing Co.: Mail Order Secrets**
  http://plateaubiz.com?linkpage

- **Relocatable Business Newsletter**
  http://relocatable.com

- **Sales Doctors, Inc.**
  http://www.salesdoctors.com

- **Small Business Administration**
  http://www.sba.gov

- **Small Business Book Mart**
  http://talkbiz.combooks/banner2.html

- **Small Business Power Tools Direct Marketing and Internet Marketing Manuals and Software**
  http://www.palis.comindex.htm

- **Target Marketing**
  http://www2.targetonline.comtm/tmcover.html

- **U.S. Government Printing Office**
  http://www.gpo.gov

- **U.S. Direct Marketing Association**
  http://www.the-dma.org

- **Yahoo! Direct Marketing**
  http://dir.yahoo.comBusiness_and_Economy/Companies/Marketing/Direct_Marketing/Direct_Mail/

- **Yahoo! Mailing Lists**
  http://dir.yahoo.comBusiness_and_Economy/Companies/Marketing/Direct_Marketing/Direct_Mail/Mailing_Lists

••• Related Sites •••

◆ **Benefit Specialists, Inc.**
http://www.ruwealthy.com

◆ **How to**
http://www.health-net.comhowto

◆ **Icemall—Mail order index**
http://www.icemall.comreports/mail_order.html

◆ **Internet Biz Stuff**
http://www.yuboo.comhowto

◆ **Kashflowz.com**
http://www.kashflowz.comarticles

◆ **ReportNet: Mail Order Business**
http://www.reportnet.netmailorder.htm

◆ **Transglobal Enterprises**
http://www.transglobalenterprises.com

◆ **200 Money Making Folios**
http://spiralup.comfolios/report-l.htm

••• MLM companies •••

◆ **Amway**
http://www.amway.com

◆ **Antique Trader**
http://www.csmonline.comantiquetrader

◆ **Autograph Times**
http://www.celebrityconnection.comfree.htm

- **Avon Products, Inc.**
  http://avon.avon.comshowpage.asp?thepage=homepage1

- **Coin World**
  http://www.coinworld.com

- **Collectors News**
  http://collectors-news.com

- **Doll Castle News**
  http://www.dollcastlenews.com

- **Fuller Brush Company**
  http://www.fullerbrush.com

- **Herbalife International, Inc.**
  http://www.herbalife.com

- **Mary Kay Cosmetics**
  http://www.marykay.com

- **Nu Skin Enterprises**
  http://www.nuskin.net

- **Rexall Sundown, Inc.**
  http://www.rexallsundown.com

- **Shaklee Corporation**
  http://www.shaklee.com

- **Sunrider International**
  http://www.sunrider.com

Whatever you need to know, we've made it E-Z!

Informative text and forms you can fill out on-screen.* From personal to business, legal to leisure—we've made it E-Z!

Get Out Of Debt

Credit Repair

Vital Records

Personal & Family

For all your family's needs, we have titles that will help keep you organized and guide you through most every aspect of your personal life.

Living Wills
Includes Power of Attorney for Healthcare

Asset Protection

Buying/Selling Your Home

Business

Whether you're starting from scratch with a home business or you just want to keep your corporate records in shape, we've got the programs for you.

Incorporation

Corporate Records

Accounting

Your Profitable Home Business

Selling on the Web

Advertising Your Business

* Not all topics include forms   ss 2001.r1

Made E·Z® Library

Made E-Z Guides

Each comprehensive guide contains all the information y[...] need to master one of dozens of topics, plus sample forms [...] applicable).

Most guides also include an appendix of valuable resource[...] a handy glossary, and the valuable 14-page supplement "H[...] to Save on Attorney Fees."

Advertising Your Business Made E-Z G327
Learn the secrets and use the tools of the professionals.

Asset Protection Made E-Z G320
Shelter your property from financial disaster.

Bankruptcy Made E-Z G300
Take the confusion out of filing bankruptcy.

Business Startups Made E-Z G344
Plan and start any home-based or small business.

Buying/Selling a Business Made E-Z G321
Position your business and structure the deal for quick results.

Buying/Selling Your Home Made E-Z G311
Buy or sell your home for the right price—right now.

Collecting Child Support Made E-Z G315
Enforce your rights as a single parent.

Credit Repair Made E-Z G303
All the tools to put you back on track.

Divorce Made E-Z G302
Proceed on your own, without a lawyer.

Employment Law Made E-Z G312
A handy reference for employers and employees.

Financing Your Business Made E-Z G322
Negotiate the best financing and grow your business.

Free Legal Help Made E-Z G339
Enforce your rights—without an expensive lawyer.

Free Stuff For Everyone Made E-Z G347
A complete roadmap to fabulous freebies.

Fund Raising Made E-Z G332
Magnetize big donations with simple ideas.

Get Out of Debt Made E-Z
Learn how to become debt-free.

Incorporation Made E-Z G301
Information you need to incorporate your company.

Last Will & Testament Made E-Z G307
Write a will the right way—the E-Z way.

Limited Liability Companies Made E-Z G316
Learn all about the hottest new business entity.

Living Trust Made E-Z G305
Trust us to help you provide for your loved ones.

Living Will Made E-Z G306
Take steps now to insure Death With Dignity.

Marketing Your Small Business Made E-Z G335
Proven marketing strategies for business success.

Money For College Made E-Z G334
Finance your college education—without the debt!

Multi-level Marketing Made E-Z G338
Turn your own product or service into an MLM empire.

Mutual Fund Investing Made E-Z G343
Build a secure future with fast-growth mutual funds.

Offshore Investing Made E-Z G337
Transfer your wealth offshore for financial privacy.

Owning a No-Cash-Down Business Made E-Z G336
Financial independence without risk, cash, or experience.

Partnerships Made E-Z G318
Avoid double taxation.

Profitable Mail Order Made E-Z G323
Turn virtually any product into a profitable mail order item.

SBA Loans Made E-Z G325
In-depth explanation of required and optional forms.

Selling On The Web Made E-Z G324
Wealth-building, web-building strategies for any size busines[...]

Shoestring Investing Made E-Z G330
Amass more wealth with investments through strategic inves[...]

Stock Market Investing Made E-Z G331
Pick the best stocks and manage your own portfolio.

Solving Business Problems Made E-Z G326
Identify and solve business problems with proven strategies.

Solving IRS Problems Made E-Z G319
Settle with the IRS for pennies on the dollar.

Successful Resumes Made E-Z G346
Exploit your strengths, gain confidence, and secure that drea[...]

Winning Business Plans Made E-Z G342
Attract more capital—faster.

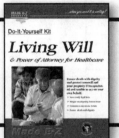

	ITEM #	QTY.	PRICE‡	EXTENSION
Made E-Z Software				
E-Z Construction Estimator	SS4300		$24.95	
E-Z Contractors' Forms	SS4301		$24.95	
Contractors' Business Builder Software Bundle	SS4002		$49.95	
Corporate Secretary	SS4003		$24.95	
Asset Protection Made E-Z	SS4304		$24.95	
Corporate Records Made E-Z	SS4305		$24.95	
Vital Records Made E-Z	SS4306		$24.95	
Managing Employees	SS4307		$24.95	
Accounting Made E-Z	SS4308		$24.95	
Limited Liability Companies (LLC)	SS4309		$24.95	
Partnerships	SS4310		$24.95	
Solving IRS Problems	SS4311		$24.95	
Winning In Small Claims Court	SS4312		$24.95	
Collecting Unpaid Bills Made E-Z	SS4313		$24.95	
Selling On The Web (E-Commerce)	SS4314		$24.95	
Your Profitable Home Business Made E-Z	SS4315		$24.95	
Get Out Of Debt Made E-Z	SS4317		$24.95	
E-Z Business Lawyer Library	SS4318		$49.95	
E-Z Estate Planner	SS4319		$49.95	
E-Z Personal Lawyer Library	SS4320		$49.95	
Payroll Made E-Z	SS4321		$24.95	
Personal Legal Forms and Agreements	SS4322		$24.95	
Business Legal Forms and Agreements	SS4323		$24.95	
Employee Policies and Manuals	SS4324		$24.95	
Incorporation Made E-Z	SW1176		$24.95	
Last Wills Made E-Z	SW1177		$24.95	
Everyday Law Made E-Z	SW1185		$24.95	
Everyday Legal Forms & Agreements Made E-Z	SW1186		$24.95	
Business Startups Made E-Z	SW1192		$24.95	
Credit Repair Made E-Z	SW2211		$24.95	
Business Forms Made E-Z	SW2223		$24.95	
Buying and Selling A Business Made E-Z	SW2242		$24.95	
Marketing Your Small Business Made E-Z	SW2245		$24.95	
Get Out Of Debt Made E-Z	SW2246		$24.95	
Winning Business Plans Made E-Z	SW2247		$24.95	
Successful Resumes Made E-Z	SW2248		$24.95	
Solving Business Problems Made E-Z	SW2249		$24.95	
Profitable Mail Order Made E-Z	SW2250		$24.95	
Deluxe Business Forms	SW2251		$49.95	
E-Z Small Business Library	SW2252		$49.95	
Sub-total for Software			**$**	
Made E-Z Guides				
Bankruptcy Made E-Z	G300		$14.95	
Incorporation Made E-Z	G301		$14.95	
Divorce Made E-Z	G302		$14.95	
Credit Repair Made E-Z	G303		$14.95	
Living Trusts Made E-Z	G305		$14.95	
Living Wills Made E-Z	G306		$14.95	
Last Will & Testament Made E-Z	G307		$14.95	
Buying/Selling Your Home Made E-Z	G311		$14.95	
Employment Law Made E-Z	G312		$14.95	
Collecting Child Support Made E-Z	G315		$14.95	
Limited Liability Companies Made E-Z	G316		$14.95	
Partnerships Made E-Z	G318		$14.95	
Solving IRS Problems Made E-Z	G319		$14.95	
Asset Protection Made E-Z	G320		$14.95	
Buying/Selling A Business Made E-Z	G321		$14.95	
Financing Your Business Made E-Z	G322		$14.95	
Profitable Mail Order Made E-Z	G323		$14.95	
Selling On The Web Made E-Z	G324		$14.95	
SBA Loans Made E-Z	G325		$14.95	
Solving Business Problems Made E-Z	G326		$14.95	
Advertising Your Business Made E-Z	G327		$14.95	
Shoestring Investing Made E-Z	G330		$14.95	
Stock Market Investing Made E-Z	G331		$14.95	
Fund Raising Made E-Z	G332		$14.95	
Money For College Made E-Z	G334		$14.95	
Marketing Your Small Business Made E-Z	G335		$14.95	

‡ Prices are for a single item, and are subject to change without notice.

continued on nex

	ITEM #	QTY.	PRICE‡	EXTENSION
Owning A No-Cash-Down Business Made E-Z	G336		$14.95	
Offshore Investing Made E-Z	G337		$14.95	
Multi-level Marketing Made E-Z	G338		$14.95	
Get Out Of Debt Made E-Z	G340		$14.95	
Your Profitable Home Business Made E-Z	G341		$14.95	
Winning Business Plans Made E-Z	G342		$14.95	
Mutual Fund Investing Made E-Z	G343		$14.95	
Business Startups Made E-Z	G344		$14.95	
Successful Resumes Made E-Z	G346		$14.95	
Free Stuff For Everyone Made E-Z	G347		$14.95	
Sub-total for Guides			$	
Made E-Z Kits				
Bankruptcy Kit	K300		$24.95	
Incorporation Kit	K301		$24.95	
Divorce Kit	K302		$24.95	
Credit Repair Kit	K303		$24.95	
Living Trust Kit	K305		$24.95	
Living Will Kit	K306		$24.95	
Last Will & Testament Kit	K307		$19.95	
Buying and Selling Your Home Kit	K311		$24.95	
Employment Law Kit	K312		$24.95	
Limited Liability Company Kit	K316		$24.95	
Business Startups Kit	K320		$24.95	
Small Business/Home Business Kit	K321		$24.95	
Sub-total for Kits			$	
Made E-Z Books				
Everyday Legal Forms & Agreements Made E-Z	BK407		$24.95	
Personnel Forms Made E-Z	BK408		$24.95	
Collecting Unpaid Bills Made E-Z	BK409		$24.95	
Corporate Records Made E-Z	BK410		$24.95	
Everyday Law Made E-Z	BK411		$24.95	
Vital Records Made E-Z	BK412		$24.95	
Business Forms Made E-Z	BK414		$24.95	
Sub-total for Books			$	
Labor Law Posters				
☆ Federal Labor Law	LP001		$14.95	
☆ State Specific Labor Law see state listings below			$39.95	

State	Item#	QTY	State	Item#	QTY	State	Item#	QTY
AL	83801		KY	83817		ND	83834	
AK	83802		LA	83818		OH	83835	
AZ	83803		ME	83819		OK	83836	
AR	83804		MD	83820		OR	83837	
CA	83805		MA	83821		PA	83838	
CO	83806		MI	83822		RI	83839	
CT	83807		MN	83823		SC	83840	
DE	83808		MS	83824		S. Dakota not available		
DC	83848		MO	83825		TN	83842	
FL	83809		MT	83826		TX	83843	
GA	83810		NE	83827		UT	83844	
HI	83811		NV	83828		VT	83845	
ID	83812		NH	83829		VA	83846	
IL	83813		NJ	83830		WA	83847	
IN	83814		NM	83831		WV	83849	
IO	83815		NY	83832		WI	83850	
KS	83816		NC	83833		WY	83851	

☆ Required by Federal & State Laws

Sub-total for Posters	$
TOTAL FOR ALL PRODUCTS	$
Add Shipping & Handling $3.50 for first item, $1.50 for each additional item	$
TOTAL PRODUCTS and S & H	$
Florida Residents add 6% sales tax	$
TOTAL OF ORDER	$

‡ *Prices are for a single item, and are subject to change without notice.*

MADE E-Z
P R O D U C T S

Name

Company

Position

Address

City

State   Zip

Phone
(   )

PAYMENT
❏ check enclosed, payable to:
Made E-Z Products, Inc.
384 S. Military Trail
Deerfield Beach, FL 33442

❏ charge my credit card: ❏ MasterCard ❏ VISA

ACCOUNT NO.   EXP. DATE

Signature: (required for credit card purchases)

By the book...

MADE E-Z™ *books provide all the forms you need to take care of business and save on legal fees –*
only $24.95 each!

Everyday Legal Forms & Agreements Made E-Z *Stock No. BK407*
A do-it-yourself legal library of 301 ready-to-use perforated legal documents for virtually every personal or business need!

Corporate Records Made E-Z *Stock No. BK410*
Keep your own corporate records current and in compliance... without a lawyer!

Personnel Forms Made E-Z *Stock No. BK408*
Over 240 documents to manage your employees more efficiently and legally!

Vital Records Made E-Z *Stock No. BK412*
201 simple and ready-to-use forms to help you keep organized records for your family, your business and yourself!

Collecting Unpaid Bills Made E-Z *Stock No. BK409*
Essential for anyone who extends credit and needs an efficient way to collect.

Business Forms Made E-Z *Stock No. BK414*
Instantly organize and track important administrative and planning functions to more efficiently operate your business.

ss 2001.r2

Index